W9-AXL-403

6 Amazing Bible Stories to Strangely Warm Our Hearts

JAMES W. MOORE

6 Amazing Bible Stories to Strangely Warm Our Hearts

IDEAL FOR USE WITH
The WESLEY STUDY BIBLE

Abingdon Press
Nashville

6 AMAZING BIBLE STORIES TO STRANGELY WARM OUR HEARTS

Copyright © 2011 by Abingdon Press

All rights reserved.

No part of this work may be reproduced or transmitted in any form or by any means, electronic or mechanical, including photocopying and recording, or by any information storage or retrieval system, except as may be expressly permitted by the 1976 Copyright Act or in writing from the publisher. Requests for permission should be addressed to Permissions, United Methodist Publishing House, P.O. Box 801, Nashville, TN 37202-0801, or emailed to permissions@umpublishing.org.

This book is printed on acid-free paper.

Library of Congress Cataloging-in-Publication Data

Moore, James W. (James Wendell), 1938-
  6 amazing Bible Stories to strangely warm our hearts / James W. Moore.
    p. cm.
  ISBN 978-1-4267-1589-1 (pbk. : alk. paper)
  1. Christian life—Methodist authors. 2. Christian life—Textbooks. 3. Bible—Textbooks. I. Title. II. Title: Six amazing Bible Stories to strangely warm our hearts.
  BV4511.M66 2011
  248.4'87—dc22

                                                                    2011004791

All scripture quotations are taken from the New Revised Standard Version of the Bible, copyright 1989, Division of Christian Education of the National Council of the Churches of Christ in the United States of America. Used by permission. All rights reserved.

Excerpts taken from *The Wesley Study Bible* © 2009 by Abingdon Press; Joel B. Green and William H. Willimon, General Editors. Used by permission.

11 12 13 14 15 16 17 18 19 20—10 9 8 7 6 5 4 3 2 1

MANUFACTURED IN THE UNITED STATES OF AMERICA

For June,
every day a
miracle

CONTENTS

HOW TO READ THE BIBLE

Some years ago, I had a youth minister on my staff named Tim, who was quite a character. He and his family were a situation comedy looking for a place to happen. A case in point is what happened to them one Friday evening. They returned home late to discover that their dog, Dallas, had somehow gotten through the backyard fence and was lost somewhere out there in the neighborhood. Good father and dog lover that he is, Tim dutifully went out into the night in search of Dallas the dog.

As he walked the streets of Houston at 1:00 a.m., calling, "Dallas! Dallas!" a Houston police officer thought he sounded strange and looked suspicious. He stopped Tim and asked him who he was and what he was doing. Tim explained, and the police officer was most sympathetic. After getting a description of the dog, the policeman promised Tim that he would watch for him as he made his patrols through the neighborhood.

Tim continued the search a little while longer with no luck and finally gave up for the night, went home, and went to bed. But at 3:30 a.m., the front door bell rang loudly. Tim sprang out of bed and ran to answer the door in his T-shirt and boxer shorts. It was the police officer, who said, "Tim, I think I found your dog. Come quick. Get in the squad car and let's check it out."

Tim ran out in his T-shirt and boxer shorts and jumped into the police car, and off they went. Sure enough, it was their dog, Dallas. They caught him, put him in the police car, and headed back toward home. Suddenly, the radio in the police car crackled, and a dispatcher told the police officer to go as soon as possible to an address on Riverview Drive to investigate a disturbance there.

"Hey! Wait a minute," said Tim. "That's my house. That's my address."

The policeman called the dispatcher and asked the nature of the problem at that residence. The dispatcher said, "A lady called and said her front door bell rang at 3:30 a.m. Her husband went to answer it and never returned. She said she heard the front door slam, and she thinks her husband has been kidnapped—in his underwear!"

Now, I told you that they are a situation comedy looking for a place to happen. Soon everything was cleared up and straightened out. And as they say, "All's well that ends well." But there is a point here worth noting, namely, this: sometimes we can get so mixed up. Things can get so

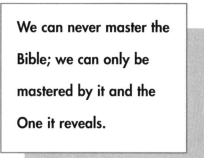

We can never master the Bible; we can only be mastered by it and the One it reveals.

complicated for us. Even when our intentions are the best, we can get confused and mixed up.

It's true in our life experiences, and it is also uniquely true with the Bible. We can get so confused and perplexed about the Bible. We can get so mixed up by people who claim to know the Bible. This is especially true if we don't know what the Scriptures are or how to approach them. The truth is that very few people really know how to read the Bible. Some, in desperation, have turned to the Scriptures for strength, for comfort, for answers, for the word of life—only to come up empty because they don't know how to find its treasures. You see, the person who is looking for a way to master the Bible in three easy lessons will always be disappointed.

In the first place, we can never master the Bible; we can only be mastered by it and the One it reveals. In the second place, the Bible is so immeasurably rich that the human mind cannot possibly embrace it all in a few feeble attempts.

> **How do we read the Bible so that it really comes alive for us?**

So the question is this: How do we read the Bible so that it really comes alive for us? How can we let its great truths touch us, inspire us, stretch us, change us, and warm our hearts? How can it bring us to a deeper relationship with God and a deeper understanding of God and what he means life to be? How do we read the Bible without getting bogged down, lost, discouraged, or confused?

We joke a lot about the Bible and our lack of knowledge regarding it. Remember the one about the college student who was asked on an exam to name the four Gospels. He answered Jesus, Moses, Buddha, and Confusion.

Or how about the little boy who was asked in Sunday school to draw a picture of something in the biblical account of the Christmas story. He turned in a picture of an airplane with four heads in the cockpit. When the teacher asked about it, he explained that it was Mary, Joseph, and the baby Jesus on their flight to Egypt.

"But who is the fourth head?" the teacher asked. The little boy answered, "That's Pontius the Pilot!"

One of my favorites is about the young minister who was told by an older minister that if he ever forgot the marriage ceremony, he should not panic but just quote Scripture verses until he remembered the ritual. Sure enough, at his very first wedding, the young minister went blank, and as the bride and groom stood there before him, he blurted out the only Scripture verse he could think of at that moment, "Father, forgive them; for they do not know what they are doing" (Luke 23:34).

We laugh and joke about it, but the truth is that our biblical illiteracy is no joke; it is no laughing matter. Actually, we need to be very careful as we read and study the Bible.

Let me show you what I mean. Recall 1 John 4:18. You will find there this beautiful verse: "There is no fear in love, but perfect love casts out fear." Now imagine that we want to send a telegram of congratulations to a young woman who has just gotten married. To save money, we tell the operator to simply have the telegram read 1 John 4:18. But suppose the telegraph operator doesn't know very much about the Bible, so she carelessly leaves off the numeral *1*. So, when our friend receives the telegram, she turns not to 1 John 4:18 but to John 4:18.

When you look at John 4:18, you will see that instead of reading, "There is no fear in love, but perfect love casts out fear," she reads, "You have had five husbands, and the one you have now is not your husband."

The point is clear. When we read the Bible, we need to know what we are doing. As the Bible puts it, "All scripture is inspired by God and is useful for teaching . . . for training in righteousness" (2 Timothy 3:16), but we have to know how to approach it.

To really discover the great truths of the Bible, I have found it very helpful to do two things.

1. STUDY THE BIBLE IN CONTEXT WITH THE HIGHEST LEVEL OF ACADEMIC INTEGRITY

That is, raise crucial questions like these:

Who wrote this?
When was it written?
Why was it written?
To whom was it written?
What did the words mean back then?
Where does it appear in the Bible?

In other words, read it in context.

Only when we understand the context can we get to the heart of the message.

Have you heard about the young man in Atlanta who wanted to fly to Memphis? Of course, we know the context. We know that Atlanta is in the eastern time zone and Memphis is in the central time zone, but the young man was not aware of that, so there was a little misunderstanding.

He went to the Atlanta airport and asked if they had a flight to Memphis. The ticket agent said, "Yes, it leaves at 9:00." The young man asked, "What time does it get there?" The agent answered, "9:01." "Wait a minute," said the young man. "Let me get this straight. It leaves Atlanta at 9:00 and gets to Memphis at 9:01." "That's right," said the ticket agent. "Do you want a ticket?" The young man replied, "No, but I sure want to see that thing take off!!"

You see, we need to understand the context. Studying the Bible in context is a good way to read the Bible, but the only problem is that it is incomplete. It's helpful; but alone, it's not enough because God is not subject matter. He is our living Lord. This brings us to the second key to unlocking the great truths of the Bible.

2. APPROACH THE BIBLE PERSONALLY

Read the Bible in the first person, seeing it as a personal letter from God written to you and asking:

What is this saying to me?

What is God saying to me through this passage of Scripture?

How can this help my life at this particular time?

The fatal error that many people make is that they read the Bible as spectators rather than as participants. Only when each of us becomes a participant in the drama of redemption does the Bible really come alive for us.

Remember how someone once put it: "The Bible becomes the word of God not when we get hold of it, but when it gets hold of us." I would like to suggest that a combination of these two approaches, combining the academic with the personal, is the best way to read the Bible, asking, What did this mean back then? and then asking, What does it mean right now for me? You see, it's good to ask, Why did Judas betray? But then it helps to ask, Why do I? Why do I betray Jesus?

It's good to raise the question, Why did Peter deny? But for the Bible to become the word of God for me, I also have to ask, Why do I deny my Lord? When Amos thunders out to the people of Bethel that they are guilty of wrongdoing, we hear him speaking to us as well. He is not just telling us what was wrong in Bethel. He is also telling us what is wrong in Houston or Dallas or Portland or Grover's Corners or wherever we may be living.

This means that when Jesus asks, "Who do you say that I am?" he isn't just asking his disciples long ago; he is asking you and me right here and now. When Jesus says, "Come unto me," or "Woe unto you," he is not just talking to people long ago and far away. He is speaking directly and personally to us right here and right now. Or when we read something like the story of Zacchaeus, we need to ask the academic questions:

Who was Zacchaeus?

Why was he despised?

What was going on in Jericho then?

Who were these tax collectors?

Why did Jesus go to him?

Why is this found only in Luke?

What did this mean back then?

But we can't stop there. We have to get personal and ask, Now what does it mean to me? It's then that we see that we are Zacchaeus! We are up a tree. We need Christ to come into our lives and turn us around like that, and he can do it. When we read the Bible academically, as a student wanting to learn, and personally, as a child of God wanting to obey, that's when the Bible really becomes the word of God for us. So we come to the Bible in the spirit of the hymn writer Adelaide A. Pollard as she wrote these words:

Have thine own way, Lord.

Have thine own way.

Thou art the Potter.

I am the clay.

Mold me and make me after thy will.

While I am waiting, yielded and still.

It is my hope and prayer that as we study these six amazing scriptures together our hearts may be strangely warmed.

Throughout the *Wesley Study Bible*, there are Wesleyan Core Terms and Life Application Topics that appear as sidebars within the notes. They are listed by biblical book and in alphabetical order in the back of the *Wesley Study Bible*. For your convenience at the end of each chapter of this book, you will find a Wesleyan Core Term and a Life Application Topic highlighted, with others listed for further study. Just as John Wesley, the founder of Methodism, sought to speak as plainly as possible, these brief explanations will help you live out your faith with a warmed heart and active hands.

In addition, at the end of each chapter you will find reflection questions that are suitable for self-directed or group study.

God's grace is truly amazing, and it is my hope that this book will help lead you to a deeper, richer, even more amazing faith.

CHAPTER ONE

AMAZING POWER OF LOVE

If I speak in the tongues of mortals and of angels, but do not have love, I am a noisy gong or a clanging cymbal. And if I have prophetic powers, and understand all mysteries and all knowledge, and if I have all faith, so as to remove mountains, but do not have love, I am nothing. If I give away all my possessions, and if I hand over my body so that I may boast, but do not have love, I gain nothing.

Love is patient; love is kind; love is not envious or boastful or arrogant or rude. It does not insist on its own way; it is not irritable or resentful; it does not rejoice in wrongdoing, but rejoices in the truth. It bears all things, believes all things, hopes all things, endures all things.

1 Corinthians 13:1-7

* * * *

A few years ago the Public Broadcasting System did a fascinating four-part television series *Power Politics in Washington, D.C.* The series, which ran for four consecutive nights, was based on Hedrick Smith's successful book *The Power Game.* It was an eye-opening dissection of where the power is in our nation's capital. The opening segment examined Congress. It revealed that today's officeholders have had much of their strength depleted by becoming victims of what is called "The Constant Campaign," which suggests that members of Congress are always running for office. They have to give so much time, effort, and energy to politicking that it takes away from their strength in addressing the political problems. California Congressman George Miller put it bluntly, "Before you can save the world, you have to save your seat!"

The second program in the series gave a somewhat chilling look inside the Pentagon and the sobering power struggles and skirmishes going on there constantly.

The third episode was titled "The Unelected." It revealed the awesome power that the lobbyists, the congressional staff members, and the media have in running our country. Their impact is absolutely amazing, though not always so visible or obvious. For example, in the series, Senator Tom

Eagleton suggested that ABC newsman Ted Koppel was much more powerful than any one member of the United States Senate!

The final program in the series dealt with the president, his power, and the strong influence of the people who have access to him. I was fascinated by this PBS presentation because it not only gave an inside view of Washington and how it works, but it also revealed how obsessed we in our modern world have become with power.

In his book *The Power of Love*, Dr. D. L. Dykes talked about this. He said,

We are a people who live in a time almost totally dedicated to the concept of power. *We love power.* If we are to believe the television commercials, we even want our detergents to have *"bulldozer power."* We want automobiles with 400-horsepower engines, capable of cruising at 120 miles an hour, when we know we have to drive in zones from 35 to 65 miles an hour. For the most part, our greatest sense of security is in believing that we are the strongest nation in the world . . . and we can sleep peacefully at night because of that sense of security. Power is a watchword of our time. (D. L. Dykes, *The Power of Love* [Nashville: Abingdon Press, 1988], p. 13)

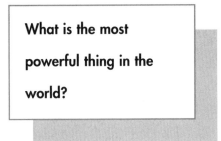

What is the most powerful thing in the world?

But now let me ask you something. What is the most powerful thing in the world? What is the strongest thing on earth? Is it force? Is it military might? Is it political clout? Is it oratory? Is it influence? Is it money? Is it position? How would you answer that question? What is the most powerful thing in the world?

Nels Ferre, one of the great theologians of our time, helps us answer that question by relating a true experience from his early life. He was something of a child prodigy. Early on, his family and the school officials in his homeland of Sweden realized that he was gifted. He was so bright! Because of his brilliance, he was selected at age thirteen to come to America to study. Even his departure from Sweden was an unforgettable experience, which he vividly recalled.

The family had prayer, and each of the eight children prayed. When they finished, they walked together to the railroad station. Dr. Ferre said that as they stood there waiting for the train, his brothers and sisters were all wishing him well, and his father was giving fatherly advice. His

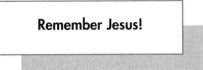

Remember Jesus!

mother hugged him tightly and tried to say something, but then her eyes welled up with tears and her voice choked away to nothing. What does a mother say to her thirteen-year-old son who is going off for a long time to another country thousands of miles away? What would you say to your child?

Nels Ferre said, "I could see Mother, her mouth forming words and not being able to say anything." Finally, the conductor blew his whistle, young Nels Ferre got on board, and the train began to pull away. He looked out the train window and waved good-bye to his family. As his eyes began to fill with tears, he turned and stared down at the floor. But suddenly, something told him to look back. As the train was slowly pulling out of the station, he glanced back and saw his mother running frantically alongside the train and motioning for him to open the window. Quickly, he opened the window, and he heard his mother shouting as she ran alongside the train, her final words of instruction to him: "Nels, remember Jesus! Remember Jesus!"

What is the most powerful thing in the world? Nels Ferre's mother knew the answer to that. The strongest thing in the world is the spirit of Jesus Christ! The spirit of Christ is more powerful than money, more powerful than position, more powerful than military might.

Even the renowned French general Napoleon came to realize that. Early in his career he was reported to have said, "God is on the side of the ones who have the biggest guns." Later, he said, "Caesar, Alexander, and I built our

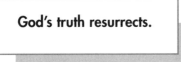

God's truth resurrects.

empires on might, while Jesus built His kingdom on love and today millions of people all over the world will bow at the mention of His name."

The spirit of Christ is the strongest thing in the world because it is of God. It is simply indestructible. You can't kill God's truth. It resurrects! You can't stop God's word. It will not be silenced! You can't destroy God's righteousness. It will ultimately win!

If you want to know what God is like and if you want to know what God wants us to be like, remember Jesus!

If you want to do right and be right and stand for what is right and come out on the side of right—remember Jesus! If you want to know the greatest power this world has ever seen—remember Jesus! Empires will rise and fall; military establishments will conquer and be conquered; leaders will come and go; but his truth will keep marching on!

When we remember Jesus—who he was, what he believed in, how he lived, and what he taught—many things come to mind. But here are three that will give us power to love and live in these challenging days.

1. HOPE IS BETTER THAN DESPAIR

Jesus showed us that hope is better than despair. The life of Jesus planted the indomitable spirit of hope deep in our souls. Hope means life and light. Despair means death and darkness. Hope is the energy, the fuel, the power source that keeps us going, while despair takes the wind out of our sails.

Some time back, the gas gauge on my car went haywire. It started moving constantly back and forth like a miniature windshield wiper. Needless to say, that was not a lot of help in telling me how much—or how little—gas I had left in the tank. But while the gas gauge was acting up, I had to make a trip and drive to Buffalo, Texas. I knew that I was getting low on gas because I had driven more than three hundred miles since my last fill-up. But you know, all men seem to have two things in common when it comes to traveling. First, we don't like to stop to ask directions, and second, we don't like to stop for gas. We want to hurry up and get where we are going and set a new record or something. Anyway, as I came into Buffalo, my car began to hesitate and bump and sputter and try to quit. Fortunately, I was able to coast into a service station. As you might suspect, there was nothing wrong with the car. It was in good shape, relatively new, well tuned. There was nothing wrong, except that like all cars, it would not run without fuel. It would not run without energy; it would not run without gas.

Our lives are like that, and hope in God is our energy

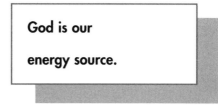

God is our energy source.

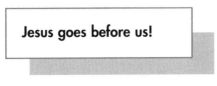

Jesus goes before us!

source. It's the gasoline that empowers us. Take it away and we quit and sputter and die.

A frontiersman came one day to a lake that was frozen over. He needed to cross the lake, but he was afraid. How solidly frozen was the ice? Would it hold him? In his fear, he knelt down and began to crawl timidly on his hands and knees, listening intently for any sound that might signal to him that the ice was breaking. Suddenly, he heard a happy sound, a reassuring sound. It was a team of horses pulling a wagon. They were in the middle of the frozen lake, moving rapidly. The frontiersman knew then that if the ice could support a horse-drawn wagon, it surely could support him. He stood confidently to his feet and boldly continued his journey across the lake with a feeling of great exhilaration.

That is the good news of our Christian faith. That is the power of the gospel. One has gone before us! He has shown us that the ice will hold us. That is Christian hope, and there is great power in that. Hope is better than despair.

2. FORGIVENESS IS BETTER THAN VENGEANCE

Jesus taught that, and he was right! I don't know of anything more life depleting than vengeance. That attitude can absolutely devastate our souls. On the other side of the coin, I don't know of anything more powerful—or more life giving—than forgiveness.

Paul Scherer was a highly regarded preacher for many years at Trinity Lutheran Church in New York City. Toward the beginning of Scherer's ministry at Trinity, Harry Emerson Fosdick, who was the minister at Riverside Church, sent a letter to his ministerial colleagues in Manhattan concerning a certain social issue. Paul Scherer received the letter, disagreed with Fosdick, and wrote a hot letter back to him. In addition to attacking Fosdick's position, Paul Scherer attacked Fosdick harshly and personally. As a result of this hard confrontation, Paul Scherer felt that he could never again even speak to Fosdick.

Several months later, Dr. Scherer attended a convocation at Union Seminary. As he settled into his seat, he glanced at the bulletin and saw that the speaker was to be Dr. Harry Emerson Fosdick. Scherer wanted to leave, but just then the processional began and he couldn't get out graciously because he was in the aisle seat on the front pew. During the processional, while the clergy waited for the choir to get seated, Dr. Fosdick found himself standing next to Paul Scherer.

Just then an amazing thing happened. A God Thing! Dr. Fosdick reached over and gently placed his hand on Paul Scherer's right shoulder and gave it a little squeeze. Dr.

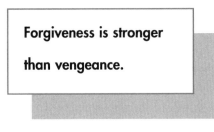

Forgiveness is stronger than vengeance.

Fosdick did not say a word, but with that squeeze, he spoke volumes. He just gently squeezed and then softly patted Dr. Scherer's shoulder and with that simple gesture, with that tender touch, suddenly, reconciliation happened! As a result of that brief but meaningful moment, Harry Emerson Fosdick and Paul Scherer became the closest of friends for the rest of their lives, showing once again that forgiveness is stronger than vengeance.

The power of forgiveness is incredible. Jesus taught us that in word and in deed. Hope is better than despair. Forgiveness is better than vengeance, and love is better than hostility.

3. LOVE IS BETTER THAN HOSTILITY

A little freckle-faced boy named Tommy had lived at an orphanage as long as he could remember. It was the custom at this home to parade the boys and girls to the parlor whenever someone came to see about adopting one of the children. Tommy had made that trip to the parlor many times, but somehow he was always one of the first to be excused. But one day a big car with a chauffeur stopped at the curb in front of the orphanage. Once again, Tommy was ushered into the parlor. And for some reason, this time he was not asked to leave. A well-dressed woman wanted to adopt

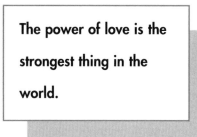

The power of love is the strongest thing in the world.

him. She said, "Tommy, if you will come home with me, you can have more than you ever dreamed possible—your own room, your own telephone, new clothes, toys, a pony."

Surprisingly, Tommy said, "Well, if that's all you have to offer, I'd just as soon stay here."

The orphanage director was a bit embarrassed, and she asked, "Why, Tommy, besides all those nice things, what on earth do you want?"

Tommy replied, "I just want someone to love me!"

More than anything, that is what we see in the spirit of Christ, the promise that someone does, indeed, love us, and the call to be a loving people!

The power of love. Stronger than hostility, stronger than fame, stronger than force, stronger than money. Remember how Paul put it, "Love never ends . . . the greatest of these is love" (1 Corinthians 13:8, 13).

* * * *

WESLEYAN CORE TERM: "HOPE"

First Peter 3:15 reminds us of the hope that is within us. One of the important contributions that Wesley made in the way we think about this hope within is the way it illumines sanctification. Hope is a this-worldly activity because it signals our interest to become more Christ-like, so it requires actively loving God and our neighbor. Wesley believed that all Christians could realize this hope while on their journey. Wesley's understanding of hope also pushes us toward an other-worldly consummation, which is the hope of eternal life. For Wesley, the hope for consummation was still a part of the sanctifying process, resulting in Christians fully recovering the image of God. Therefore, the hope of becoming more Christ-like ultimately transforms us as we grow into the image of Christ. The hope that is within us is both this-worldly and other-worldly because both are grounded in being transformed into the image of Christ.

LIFE APPLICATION TOPIC: "LOVE OF GOD"

"The LORD of hosts is mustering an army for battle" (Isaiah 13:4b). God always acts to redeem and rescue us. We can't outrun, out-give, outlast, or outgrow God's love. Out of the depth of that love, God delivered the people of God out of Egypt, moved an army to deliver the people of God from exile, and later would send the Son to rescue the world. The whole of Scripture captures God's great love affair with humanity. We may try to run and hide, but the arm of God's love for us is always long enough to reach and rescue us.

(See also the *Wesley Study Bible*: Wesleyan Core Term: "Forgiveness"; Life Application Topic: "Love One Another.")

* * * *

BIBLE STUDY EXTRA: CORINTH

Corinth is a city that commands the isthmus that links the Peloponnese to mainland Greece. Paul worked with Prisca and Aquila for eighteen months while founding the church there (from spring A.D. 50 to late summer A.D. 51, Acts 1:1-18). Paul made two subsequent visits (2 Corinthians 12:14; 13:1), on the second of which he wrote the Letter to the Romans.

The city was built on two natural terraces overlooking a vast plain, noted for its agricultural richness. From ancient times, well before Paul, Corinth was considered a wealthy city.

The history of Corinth began in the fifth millennium B.C. and came to an end when Lucius Mummius, a Roman general, destroyed it in 146 B.C. The city that Paul knew was restored in 44 B.C. by Julius Caesar and became the capital of the province. Each Roman province was governed by a proconsul, who ruled for one year, and each year the citizens elected two senior magistrates, who were the executive officers of the city, and two assistants. A first-century A.D. inscription mentions an assistant named Erastus, who is thought to be the person mentioned by Paul in Romans 16:23 and 2 Timothy 4:20.

The first colonists were ex-slaves from Greece, Syria, Judea, and Egypt. Having nothing, they began by robbing tombs to make a living. These tombs contained treasures so rich that within fifty years, some of the citizens were extremely wealthy.

The population of Corinth is not known, but it is clear that the city was extremely diverse in terms of religion and ethnicity. There were Greek cults and shrines of Apollo, Athena, Aphrodite, Asclepius, Demeter and Kore, Palaimon, and Sisyphus. There is evidence of Egyptian influence and worship of Isis and Sarapis. In addition, there was a temple dedicated to the Roman emperor. The city recognized the Jewish community as a corporation of foreigners with permanent right of residence and governed by its own officials in its internal affairs (Acts 18:15).

The ethos of Corinth can be summed up in a proverb and a myth. The proverb that was quoted by Greeks and Romans was, "Not for everyone is the voyage to Corinth." It meant that only the tough survived. The myth is that of Sisyphus (as told in Homer's *Odyssey*). Sisyphus was an ancient king of Corinth who enjoyed the success of a trickster in life, but after his death in the underworld, his task was to push a rock up a mountain. Each time he approached the summit, it slipped from his hands and he had to start again, the meaning being that life was precarious and that luck counted more than effort (from *The New Interpreter's Dictionary of the Bible* [Nashville: Abingdon Press, 2008], vol. 1, pp. 732–34).

REFLECTION QUESTIONS

1. Think about those people whom you love. How do you let them know that they are important to you?

2. Share a time when you felt God's love for you.

3. Make a list of some amazing people you know, and make a commitment to pray for them daily in the upcoming week.

CHAPTER TWO

AMAZING MARKS OF CHRIST

See what large letters I make when I am writing in my own hand! It is those who want to make a good showing in the flesh that try to compel you to be circumcised—only that they may not be persecuted for the cross of Christ. Even the circumcised do not themselves obey the law, but they want you to be circumcised so that they may boast about your flesh. May I never boast of anything except the cross of our Lord Jesus Christ, by which the world has been crucified to me, and I to the world. For neither circumcision nor uncircumcision is anything; but a new creation is everything! As for those who will follow this rule—peace be upon them, and mercy, and upon the Israel of God.

From now on, let no one make trouble for me; for I carry the marks of Jesus branded on my body.

*May the grace of our Lord Jesus Christ be with
your spirit, brothers and sisters. Amen.*

Galatians 6:11-18

* * * *

When I was a young boy, our family made a vacation trip to East Texas one summer to visit relatives there. One of the vivid memories of that trip was a tour of a Texas ranch, where we watched some cowboys hard at work branding their steers. A mark was made on each steer to dramatically and clearly signify its owner.

Something like that was done to human beings in biblical times. In New Testament times, slavery was quite common. Slaves were regarded as pieces of property, and they were marked with visible signs that indicated

- to whom they belonged,
- who their owner was, and
- who their master was.

Historians tell us that

- some slaves were marked by a brand on the forehead,
- some by a tattoo on the wrist,

- and as strange as this may sound to us today, another mark of slavery was the pierced ear.

In the time of the early church, slavery and the markings of slavery were common, familiar, and accepted practices. But what is more interesting to note is that some of the slaves were voluntary slaves—that is, they chose that way of life.

It is out of this background that Paul is speaking in the sixth chapter of Galatians when he says, "From now on, let no one make trouble for me [or question me]; for I carry the marks of Jesus branded on my body."

Here Paul is saying simply this: "Look! Can't you see? It's as plain as day. I am the slave of Christ! I bear on my body the marks of Jesus! He is my Lord and Master! I belong to him heart and soul!"

The Galatians had doubted Paul. They wondered about this one who had persecuted the Christians so arduously only a short time before. They questioned his theology, his apostleship, his authority.

In answer, Paul says to the Galatians: "Look here! Anyone can see that I belong to Christ! Christ is my owner, my Master. Christ is the Lord of my life.

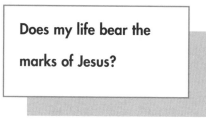

Does my life bear the marks of Jesus?

I am his property. I am his servant. I am the complete and devoted slave of Christ. He has claimed me, branded me, bought me with a price."

Paul is saying, "As surely as you can look at a group of slaves and tell by their markings to whom they belong . . . even so, you can look at me and see by my markings [by visible evidence] that I am the slave of Christ. The marks of Jesus are branded on my body!"

This raises some interesting questions for you and me, doesn't it? When people look at you and me, can they tell by our markings, by visible evidence, that we are the servants of Christ? Can they tell without question that we belong to Christ? Do we bear on our bodies the marks of Jesus?

A couple of quick comments here:

1. First, when Paul speaks of "the marks of Jesus," he is using a double analogy. He is probably referring to the physical scars that he has received on his body because of his consecration to Christ. They were physical scars from beatings, floggings, shipwrecks, exposure, and harsh persecutions, prompted by his allegiance to Christ.

2. But also remember that when Paul uses the word *body*, he doesn't mean just physical flesh. He means total personality—all that we will ever become.

So, when Paul says that he carries on his body "the marks of Jesus," he means that Christ has claimed his

> **Does all that I am reflect Christ?**

heart, his mind, his soul, his strength, his attitudes, his abilities, his whole being, his total personality. He means that the spirit of Christ pervades every aspect of his life. He means that he, in all he is and does, is the complete slave of Christ!

Let me ask you—be honest—how is it with you?

- Can people look at you today and tell by visible evidence that you are a Christian?
- Can people tell by the way you act, by the way you speak, by the way you live, and by the way you relate to others that you are the servant of Christ?
- Can people look at you and tell by the way you respond to the church, by the way you treat your mate, by the way you care for your children, by the way you act at home with your family that you have the spirit of Christ in you?

In recent years, we have seen an upsurge in the wearing of religious buttons and the displaying of religious bumper stickers. I don't know about you, but I have never much wanted to wear a sign that says, "I am a Christian." Some people do and that's okay for them, but somehow, I just don't feel comfortable wearing religious signs, probably for several reasons. For one thing, it's just not me. Then, too, I remember those hard sayings of Jesus toward the Pharisees for making a public show of religion.

I had an experience in college that affected me strongly along this line. I was visiting with a friend in his dorm room. As Ted and I were talking, suddenly the door flew open, and in charged Ted's roommate, Bill. Bill was wearing a big button that read, "I am a Christian!" in bold letters. He pulled out another button just like it, gave it to Ted, and urged him to put it on.

Ted sat there for a moment staring at that button, and then he gently placed it on his desk and said, "Bill, I appreciate you and your thoughtfulness, but I'd rather not wear the button."

"Why not?" Bill asked.

Ted responded, "Well, it's just because I feel that if I'm a Christian—really a Christian—I won't need to wear a sign. People will know it!"

What's the point? Please don't misunderstand me. I'm not putting down sign wearing necessarily. If that feels right for you, go for it—do it. I just want to underscore Ted's last comment. It has stuck in my mind over all these years: "If I'm really a Christian, I won't need to wear a sign. People will know it!"

It's okay to wear signs if we want to, but the crucial questions are these:

- Can people tell by the way we act and live that we are Christians?
- Do we in our total personalities bear the marks of Christ?

* * * *

Let me break this down a bit, be more specific, and bring it closer to home.

What are the present-day marks of discipleship? What are the marks of Christ? There are many, of course. Let me lift up a few, and I'm sure you will think of others.

1. THE HIGHEST LEVEL OF CHRISTIAN SERVICE

What is the highest level of Christian service? It's a dramatic mark of discipleship. Christians understand full well that we are the servants of Christ and that we are incomplete apart from God. We understand that God loves us, that God cares about us, and that God can use us

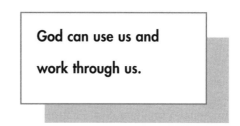

God can use us and work through us.

> **You have a lot to give.**

and work through us. Some years ago, I worked at a youth camp for senior high students. On the final night of camp, we had a consecration service that dramatically underscored this mark of discipleship. Each young person there was asked to write on a piece of paper a list of his or her unique abilities that God could use. These were put in sealed envelopes and presented at the altar in a Communion service as an act of consecration. After Communion, as persons left the tabernacle, each was given a stick that represented his or her abilities or service to God. We then moved in silence to vesper ring where a small campfire was burning. Then each camper came forward in turn and added his or her stick, which represented his or her abilities, to the fire. And when we had finished, the small campfire had become a huge bonfire.

The points of the consecration service were these:

- Every person is important in the mind of God.
- Every person has something to give.
- Every person has some contribution to make.
- Every person has some unique ability that God can use.
- Every person has something to add to the church's fire.

This is the first mark of Christ, the highest level of Christian service, the realization that God can use us as his servants, that God can take whatever abilities we may have and use them for good.

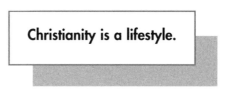

Christianity is a lifestyle.

2. THE HIGHEST LEVEL OF CHRISTIAN MORALITY

There is no question about it. We are living in a time of grave moral crisis, a time when you and I, who call ourselves Christian, can do no less than preach Christ by the way we live. The best witness is the person who lives the faith day in and day out, the one who stands tall for what is good and right and clean, the one who sees Christianity as a lifestyle—not just a creed we profess, but a life we live.

Some years ago, a student approached a professor at a prestigious university in Boston and asked the professor this question: "What does it really mean to be a Christian?" The professor realized that the student was thinking deep thoughts and was very sincere in asking the question. The professor knew that his response to the question was highly important, so carefully he began to think of how to best answer the question. As the professor was thinking through his answer, he walked over and glanced out the window of his office, and suddenly, he had his answer. He called the student over to the window

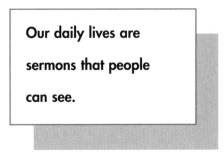

Our daily lives are sermons that people can see.

and pointed toward the campus and said, "Look there! You want to know what it really means to be a Christian. Well, there is your answer. There is Phillips Brooks!"

Dr. Phillips Brooks was one of the great preachers of his generation, who not only preached powerful sermons from his pulpit but also preached the Christian faith by the way he lived his life each day with a deep commitment to the highest level of morality. Of course, a lived-out sermon is the best and most eloquent sermon of all. This is a key mark of discipleship, isn't it? As Christians, we should stand out in a crowd by the high level of our morality, by the way we live the highest standards of righteousness. Our daily lives should be sermons that people can see.

As Christians, our morality is based on our calling to be the obedient servants of our Master. Every decision, every move, every action is measured by the Master's will. It's just at this point that we often miss the substance of Jesus' character. We are touched by his compassion and by his courage. We are inspired by his kindness and by his commitment. But we must not overlook the strong spirit of obedience to the Father's will that was so tenacious in his personality and in his morality.

Listen to him speak:

- "Your will be done, / on earth as it is in heaven" (Matthew 6:10).
- "I have come down from heaven, not to do my own will, but the will of him who sent me" (John 6:38).
- "Whoever does the will of God is my brother and sister and mother" (Mark 3:35).
- "Not my will but yours be done" (Luke 22:42).

Note that this "your will be done" theme is a key emphasis in two of our Lord's most noted prayers: the Lord's Prayer and the prayer in the Garden of Gethsemane.

There is no question about it. At the center of Jesus' ethical life was a glad and unflinching obedience to the Father's will. This kind of obedience and commitment to God's will is a key mark of discipleship and Christian morality.

In the famous St. Martin-in-the-Fields church in London there is a wonderful description of Christian morality that reads, "A Christian

Obedience and commitment to God's will are key marks of discipleship.

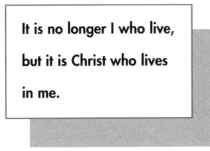

It is no longer I who live, but it is Christ who lives in me.

is a mind through which Christ thinks; a heart through which Christ loves; a voice through which Christ speaks; a hand through which Christ helps."

Paul put it like this: "It is no longer I who live, but it is Christ who lives in me" (Galatians 2:20).

First, there is the highest level of Christian service; second, there is the highest level of Christian morality. Both of these are dramatic marks of Christ. Consider one more.

3. THE HIGHEST LEVEL OF CHRISTIAN LOVE

Remember how the songwriter Peter Scholtes put it: "They'll know we are Christians by our love." It's the major mark of Christ, the key sign of discipleship.

Some years ago, a schoolteacher in Baltimore celebrated her eightieth birthday. A large crowd of former students gathered to honor her and to express their gratitude to her for what she had done in her many years of service to children and youth.

She had taught for long years in one of the city's worst sections. Before she came to the school, the rate of juvenile crime was higher there than in any other section of the city. But in time, change became noticeable because so many of her students started turning out to be good citizens—men and women of character, integrity, and leadership.

On this occasion of her eightieth birthday, doctors, lawyers, ministers, artisans, business leaders, and government officials gathered in Baltimore to say "thank you" and "happy birthday" to their teacher—this one who had touched their lives so redemptively.

A newspaper sent a reporter and a photographer to cover the event. The reporter asked the eighty-year-old teacher what her secret was. What had made her teaching so rewarding and had obviously produced so many quality leaders and good citizens?

I love her answer. She said, "Oh, I don't know. When I look at the talented young teachers in our schools today, so well prepared with training and learning, I realize how ill-prepared I was to teach. I guess I had nothing to give but love!"

What else is there to give but love? What else can you and I as Christian disciples give to God and to the people around us but the highest level of love?

When people look at us today, what do they see? Can they see the spirit of Christ in us? Can they tell

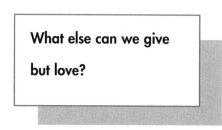

What else can we give but love?

we are committed to Christ? Do we bear in our bodies, in our total personalities, the marks of Jesus?

Do we live each day with the highest level of Christian service, the highest level of Christian morality, and the highest level of Christian love?

Paul said, "Let no one make trouble for me; for I carry the marks of Jesus branded on my body." Can you say that? Can you? Do you bear the amazing marks of Christ?

* * * *

WESLEYAN CORE TERM: "HOLINESS OF HEART"

In Jeremiah, God promises "a new covenant." God will write God's law on people's hearts. Then truly "I will be their God, and they shall be my people" (Jeremiah 31:31, 33).

Holiness of heart, not mere ceremonial holiness, has always been God's goal for his people. God intends inner transformation—the cleansing and liberating of the inmost springs of action and motivation. Jesus emphasized that evil attitudes and actions come from within (Mark 7:21-23). It is the heart, therefore, that must be cleansed.

[John] Wesley saw that "holiness of heart" could be misunderstood, however, as *solely* an interior change. The outward and ethical dimension so prominent in Scripture could be missed. So Wesley often used the phrase "inward and outward" (or "all inward and outward") holiness to forestall any disconnection between inner transformation and outward behavior. Holiness of heart means transformation by God's grace, enabling people to be holy, loving, and Christ-like in their relationships with one another and with the land.

LIFE APPLICATION TOPIC: "MARKS OF A CHRISTIAN"

Love is routinely preached. But the litmus test of this love is whether it is genuine or hypocritical, out of self-interest or putting others' well-being first.

Wesley's general rules of "doing no harm, avoiding evil, and doing good of every possible sort" are ways to help us practice love in our lives. For Wesley, faith and works are two sides of the same coin.

Wesley's "going on to perfection" requires the practice of spiritual disciplines. Love is expressed in works of piety, our devotion to God, works of mercy, and our compassionate treatment of others.

(See also the *Wesley Study Bible*: Wesleyan Core Terms: "Moral Image of God," "Image of God," and "Fruits of the Spirit"; Life Application Topics: "Grace-Filled Life" and "Discipleship.")

BIBLE STUDY EXTRA: GALATIA

Galatia was a territory in northern Asia Minor. Originally, the region was populated by Celts who migrated there from Gaul in the first half of the third century B.C. In Greek, *Galatia* (Galatians) is a variant of *Keltoi*, or Celts. In 25 B.C., the last of the Galatian kings died, leaving his kingdom in the hands of the Romans, who reorganized the area into a province by adding other districts: Isauria, parts of Lyconia, Paphlagonia, Pisidia, Phrygia, and Pontus.

Because Paul does not name any cities or towns of Galatia, it is impossible to determine whether the churches to which he wrote were in the old territory of the ethnic Galatians (north) or in the Roman provincial Galatia (south). Likewise, it is impossible to determine approximately when Paul composed his letter. At the heart of this matter is the problem of trying to coordinate portions of Galatians with seemingly parallel portions of Acts. In particular is the matter of whether Galatians 2:1-10 refers to the same events cited in Acts 15. Disagreements among scholars result in some dating Galatians as early as A.D. 49

(usually those arguing against identifying Galatians 2 with Acts 15) and others as late as A.D. 56 (those thinking that Galatians 2 and Acts 15 are different accounts of one incident). However, whenever written, the letter reflects the style that is typical of first-century Greco-Roman times.

According to Galatians 1:6, Paul wrote to the Galatians because they were deserting their confidence in his preaching and turning to what he calls a "different gospel." This other gospel was proclaimed among the Galatians by a group of outsiders who came after Paul's departure and who were probably in Galatia when Paul wrote. This false gospel was moving Galatians toward more observance of the Law. This is clear from the references in Galatians 4:10 to the calendar, in Galatians 5:2 to circumcision, and in Galatians 5:3 to the "entire law."

In order to understand what Paul is saying in Galatians, it is necessary to have an idea about who these outsiders were and what they said to cause problems. Paul says that first, they preach "another gospel" (Galatians 1:7) that is perversion of the gospel. Second, they are troubling, upsetting, and perhaps even frightening the churches. And third, these preachers in Galatia are themselves circumcised (Galatians 6:13).

From Paul, we learn that they are using the Law as a starting point and heart of their message. They probably use the phrase "the Law of Christ" because this is not a phrase Paul uses. They probably teach that God's Law was affirmed and interpreted by God's Messiah, so that Jesus is the Messiah of the Law. Their theology views the Law as primary, and they add Christ to it as an authoritative interpreter. From Paul's response, we can also understand that they probably teach that to obey the Law as interpreted by Christ is to become "descendants of Abraham" (Galatians 3:6-18).

This means that the good news as proclaimed by these other preachers was conditional. In Galatians 4:17, Paul uses the image of the gate and the gatekeepers. The preachers at Galatia have threatened to shut the Galatians out if they fail to comply with the Law. They must have understood the Law as the narrow gate to salvation and themselves as the gatekeepers who guarded the way toward a right relationship with God. This view is contrary to Paul's teachings and to Wesley's as well (from *The New Interpreter's Dictionary of the Bible*, vol. 2, pp. 508–10).

REFLECTION QUESTIONS

1. What evidence do you give in your daily life for being a Christian?

2. Read the fruit of the Spirit in Galatians 5:22-24. They are love, joy, peace, patience, kindness, generosity, faithfulness, gentleness, and self-control. In relation to these, where do you excel? Where do you need help?

3. Share a time when you saw someone witness to Christ by the way that person lives.

4. What gives you the most joy about being a Christian?

CHAPTER THREE

AMAZING DISCIPLINE

The disciples went and did as Jesus had directed them; they brought the donkey and the colt, and put their cloaks on them, and he sat on them. A very large crowd spread their cloaks on the road, and others cut branches from the trees and spread them on the road. The crowds that went ahead of him and that followed were shouting,

> *"Hosanna to the Son of David!*
>> *Blessed is the one who comes in the name of the Lord!*
> *Hosanna in the highest heaven!"*

When he entered Jerusalem, the whole city was in turmoil, asking, "Who is this?" The crowds were saying, "This is the prophet Jesus from Nazareth in Galilee."

Then Jesus entered the temple and drove out all who were selling and buying in the temple, and he

overturned the tables of the money changers and the
seats of those who sold doves. He said to them, "It is
written,

> 'My house shall be called a house of prayer';
>> but you are making it a den of robbers."

The blind and the lame came to him in the temple, and he cured them. But when the chief priests
and the scribes saw the amazing things that he did,
and heard the children crying out in the temple,
"Hosanna to the Son of David," they became angry
and said to him, "Do you hear what these are saying?" Jesus said to them, "Yes; have you never read,

> 'Out of the mouths of infants and nursing
>> babies
> you have prepared praise for yourself'?"

He left them, went out of the city to Bethany, and
spent the night there.

Matthew 21:6-17

* * * *

I want to begin this chapter like the blindfolded discus
thrower. He didn't set any records, but he kept the crowd
alert! I'm not planning to set any records, but I would like

to try to alert us to what Jesus' triumphal entry into Jerusalem on Palm Sunday was all about. It is one of the great passages in all of the Bible for a number of reasons.

First, it was an unforgettable scene. Who could ever forget the picture of Jesus riding victoriously into the city on a donkey with excited people running and spreading clothing and palm branches on the road before him and shouting joyous and loud hosannas into the air? What a sight! What an unforgettable scene!

Second, it was a dramatic moment! Jesus could not have picked a more dramatic moment. It was the Passover time, and the city was bursting at the seams with people. From far and near, they had come to celebrate this significant festival. For one reason, there was a law that required every adult male Jew who lived within twenty miles of Jerusalem to attend Passover. In addition, people from every corner of the world were there. One scholar suggests that more than two million people may have been crowded into Jerusalem that day. What a moment! Jesus knew it, and he made his dramatic entry into that city, which was surging with people, people who were keyed up with high religious expectations and hopes.

Third, the triumphal entry was packed with powerful symbols: the donkey, the palm branches, the hosannas, and the high-profile entrance. The prophets during biblical times often used symbols as a means of communicating their message. When they sensed that the people were not getting the point or did not understand their words, the prophets would act out their message with dramatic actions and symbols, which put their message into a picture that none could fail to see.

- The donkey was the symbol of one coming in peace.
- The palm branches symbolized a welcome for a king.
- The hosannas were shouts of praise, but also they were the cries of an oppressed people hungering for deliverance and screaming for help in their time of trouble. (The word *hosanna* literally means "save now.")
- And this high-profile entrance down Main Street was a symbol of Jesus' incredible courage. Remember that he was in trouble with the authorities; they were watching him like a hawk, and there was a price on his head. Some of his friends didn't want him to go into Jerusalem at all; others wanted him to slip in unseen and to hide in the shadows. But no, Jesus chose the way of courage and came in center stage, into the spotlight, proclaiming his message dramatically and powerfully.

As we read this story carefully, we realize that the triumphal entry didn't just suddenly or accidentally happen. It was intentional. It was a bold, systematic, well-thought-out plan. To get the real impact of Palm Sunday, we have to go back several days to that place in Luke 9 where Jesus "set his

face to go to Jeru-
salem" (verse 51).

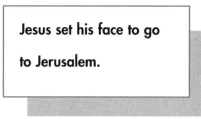

Jesus set his face to go to Jerusalem.

"He set his face
to go to Jeru-
salem." What in
the world does that
mean? In plain language it means that he made up his mind
to go to Jerusalem to strike a blow for justice. He made up
his mind to go to Jerusalem and cleanse the Temple because
he felt that the Temple—the sacred place of worship—had
somehow over the years become corrupted. It had become a
den of thieves.

Let me illustrate what that means. Imagine if you will
that your name is Nathaniel. You are a Jewish man living
eighteen miles north of Jerusalem in the time of Jesus. At
Passover, you are required by law to go to Jerusalem to participate in this holy festival in order to get God's forgiveness
not only for yourself but also for your whole family. So, as
the head of your house, you go to Jerusalem for Passover.
You walk the eighteen miles.

Once in the city you buy a lamb in the marketplace to use
as a sacrifice to get forgiveness for your family. And this is
very important; you go to the Temple, carrying your lamb.
But the authorities stop you and tell you that your lamb has
to be inspected by the Temple inspectors. You have to pay a
fee for the inspection. Can you believe it? Your lamb fails
the inspection. Oh, no! What are you going to do? I mean,

your family's forgiveness is at stake, and your reputation as a strong leader of the family clan is on the line. "No problem," the Temple authorities say. "We have some lambs over here that have already passed inspection. We will be glad to sell you one of them."

You are so relieved; that is, until you realize that the Temple lamb is priced at fifteen times what you paid for the one in the marketplace. Now look at this: you are out the money for the marketplace lamb that didn't pass inspection. You are out the money for the inspection, and now you have to buy a Temple lamb that is fifteen times more than the going marketplace rate for a lamb. But what are you going to do?

Forgiveness is at stake here, so you bite the bullet and fish into your wallet and come up with the money to pay this unfair, exorbitant price. Then the Temple authorities say, "Wait a minute. You can't use that money in here. It has the picture of Caesar on it."

"But it's all the money I've got," you say.

"No problem," they answer. "We have some money changers over here who will [are you ready for this?], for a fee, change your money into acceptable currency. And oh, by the way," they add, "while you are over there, you'd better get some more money changed so you can pay your Temple taxes too."

Jesus was infuriated by all of this. It was abuse and exploitation of these poor pilgrims, and it was a terrible misuse of the house of God. The people were being exploited at the point of their basic relationship with

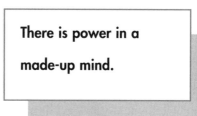

There is power in a made-up mind.

God: "Pay up or no forgiveness." This was wrong, terribly wrong. And Jesus knew it.

So he made up his mind to go to Jerusalem and speak out against it. Jesus decided, "I'm going to Jerusalem. I'm going to speak out against that, even if they kill me." And that is exactly what happened. That is exactly what he did and what they tried to do. He hit them in the pocketbook, and later they hit him with a cross. But they couldn't kill him. They couldn't silence him. God's truth always resurrects. Making up your mind—there is great power in that!

For twelve years, I was privileged to work with D. L. Dykes, one of the great preachers of America. Dr. Dykes once told a wonderful story about his mother that makes the point. When D. L. was in high school, he was a tall, lanky, long-legged boy, and his mother was quite short— well under five feet tall.

On Friday nights when D. L. got ready to go out on a date, his mother walked over to him, stood up on her tip-toes, and straightened his tie. Then she said, "D. L., have you made up your mind to be a gentleman tonight?" When D. L. answered, "Yes, Mother," a serene look spread over her face, and she was perfectly satisfied and at peace because she believed strongly that when you make up your mind, you are as good as there.

There is a lot of truth in that. For example, if you want to lose weight, it doesn't really matter which diet you choose: Weight Watchers, the South Beach Diet, the Scarsdale Diet, the Pritikin Diet, the Dolly Parton Diet—whatever. It doesn't really matter. What matters is that you make up your mind.

It's also true spiritually. We have to commit to it and set our faces toward it; we have to make up our minds. This calls for discipline, which for most of us means that we need to depend on Jesus to help us fulfill our calling to be a Christian. With these thoughts as a backdrop, let me lift up four questions.

1. HAVE YOU MADE UP YOUR MIND TO COMMIT TO THE CHURCH?

Have you made up your mind to go to church, to support the church, and to serve the church?

Some years ago, a young couple came to see me. They had a problem. They were getting into a big argument every Sunday morning about whether or not to go to church. The first Sunday back from their honeymoon, the wife said, "Let's go to church this morning." The husband thought, *I don't want to be henpecked,* so he answered, "I'm not going, and neither are you." As you can imagine, that didn't go over very well, so and round and round they went, fussing back and forth all day long.

The next Sunday, he said, "Well, let's go to church." "No way," she retorted. "You wouldn't go with me last Sunday, and I'm not going with you this Sunday." And round and round they went. Sunday after Sunday this happened for two months, and finally, they showed up in my office to talk about their problem.

I said to them, "You know, we never have that discussion at our house. That's no problem for us at all because we made that decision already—a long time ago. We made up our minds to commit to the church, to go to church. So we don't have to deal with it over and over, and that saves a lot of time and energy. Just decide once and for all to go to church, and it's settled."

Jesus never quit on the church. When we see Jesus cleansing the Temple, it looks at first glance as if he is against the church, but no, not at all. He did what he did because he loved the church and wanted to save it. He was committed to it and wanted to redeem it.

How is it with you? Have you made up your mind

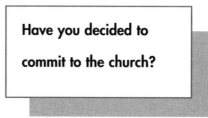

Have you decided to commit to the church?

to commit to the church? Discipline means that you are committed and have made up your mind to hold to that commitment. When the roll is called down here, will you be there?

2. HAVE YOU MADE UP YOUR MIND TO STAND TALL FOR WHAT IS RIGHT?

In his autobiography, Phil Donahue tells of the time when he was starting out as a young television reporter. He was sent to cover a mine disaster. Some miners were trapped deep down in the mine. It was late at night and freezing cold. Snow was on the ground. The rescue team was down in the mine shaft; worried relatives and friends were gathered at the opening to the mine, waiting anxiously for some word of hope. Someone began to sing, "What a friend we have in Jesus, all our sins and griefs to bear."

Voices joined in. Then it was quiet. A minister stepped out of the crowd and said, "Let us pray." It was a brief but very moving prayer. Donahue said it was such a powerful moment that he got goose bumps all over. The only problem was that it was so cold that the television camera froze up and wouldn't work. Donahue held the camera against his body and rubbed it to get it functioning again. Finally, he got it working, went to the minister, and asked him to re-create the moment and repeat the prayer for television. The minister declined, saying you can't re-create a sacred moment like that.

Donahue said, "I'm a TV reporter representing 260 stations. Millions of people will be

> **Stand tall for what is right.**

able to see you and hear your beautiful prayer." But again, the minister said no. Donahue said, "Maybe you don't understand. I'm not representing some local TV station. I'm with CBS. The whole nation will be able to see this." The old country preacher again said no and turned and walked away into the cold night.

Donahue was dumbfounded and furious. He couldn't understand it. Later it hit him. He wrote that he realized he was witnessing something special called "integrity." He wrote, "The man wouldn't showbiz for Jesus. He wouldn't sell his soul for TV, not even—praise God—for CBS." It was an easy decision for that minister because he (like Jesus) had already made up his mind to stand tall for what is right. The question is, Have we?

Standing tall for what is right can be very difficult to do. We are all prone to peer pressure, temptations, and even the impulse to take the easy way out. It takes the amazing help of God to help keep us on paths of righteousness.

3. HAVE YOU MADE UP YOUR MIND TO BE PART OF THE SOLUTION RATHER THAN PART OF THE PROBLEM?

When Jesus rode into Jerusalem on a donkey, he meant that he was coming in peace as a peacemaker. He wanted to be part of the solution.

Some years ago, our daughter, Jodi, was selected for the Homecoming Court at Louisiana Tech University. She was recognized and presented at halftime of a Saturday night football game. Of course, we had to be there for that special moment.

After the game, I began the long drive back to Houston so I could be in the pulpit on Sunday morning. All went well until I came to a small East Texas town, which shall remain nameless. It was two o'clock in the morning, and the streets were deserted. Suddenly, an old dilapidated pickup pulled out of a side street right in front of me. I swerved to the left, and since no other cars were anywhere in sight, I went on and passed him.

As I went by, I waved to the driver of the pickup. He didn't wave back. Driving on, I glanced in the rearview mirror, and by the glow of the streetlights, I saw the driver reach up and take off his farmer's hat and replace it with a policeman's hat. Then he placed a big light on the dashboard. Suddenly, the light was flashing, and the siren was screaming. I pulled over, got out of my car, and walked back toward the pickup, where I was met by the deputy sheriff of that little town. I remember thinking, *Barney Fife lives.*

> **How can you be part of the solution?**

He said, "You were going thirty-two in a twenty-five-mile-per-hour zone. What do you have to say for yourself? Where are you going, and what are you doing out at this time of night?"

After I explained my situation, I'll never forget what he said: "So, you're a preacher, huh?"

"Yes, sir."

"Well, I'm not gonna give you a ticket this time—just a warning and a lecture. A lot of people get killed on the highways every year. And you, Reverend," he said sternly, "ought to be a part of the solution, not part of the problem."

I said the best thing I could think of to say at that moment in that situation. I said, "Yes, sir." But the truth is, he was right. He was right.

Have you made up your mind to be part of the solution rather than part of the problem?

4. HAVE YOU MADE UP YOUR MIND TO TAKE UP THE TORCH OF CHRIST'S LOVING-KINDNESS?

Notice how the Scripture lesson ends. Don't miss this. After Jesus cleanses the Temple, look at what he does. He brings blind, lame, diseased, and maimed people into the

Temple, and he heals them. This is significant because back then the authorities did not permit lame, blind, and diseased people to enter the Temple. They were considered to be under God's judgment, so people shunned them, excluded them, ignored them.

Not so with Jesus—he loved them; he embraced them. With this act, he was saying that the Temple is not here to abuse the people but to help them. The Temple is not here to exploit the people but to heal them. The Temple is not here to shun the people but to save them. We are not here to use people but to love them. To paraphrase the hymn writer, they will know we are Christians when we have made up our minds to

(1) commit to the church,

(2) stand tall for what is right,

(3) be part of the solution rather than part of the problem, and

(4) take up Christ's loving, gracious ways.

The amazing thing about discipline is that we cannot do it alone. We need the support of God and our community of faith— the church. Our discipline is amazing because our strength to endure

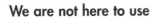
We are not here to use people but to love them.

comes not only from the Spirit working within us but also from Christian friends who stand with us.

* * * *

WESLEYAN CORE TERM: "CHARACTER OF A METHODIST"

In a small treatise, "The Character of a Methodist," published in 1742, John Wesley attempts to describe what he means by a disciple of Christ perfected in love. It is a striking portrait of noble simplicity, deeply rooted in Scripture, and dominated by the image of growth in grace and love. Wesley reflects a realistic attitude about the limitations of the human condition, but displays an even more profound optimism in what God's grace can accomplish in the life of any child desiring to walk with greater integrity in the way of the gospel. In his many subsequent publications on the theme of Christian perfection, Wesley seldom deviates from the essential portrait of the mature Christian. Those perfected in Christ "love God with all their heart, soul, mind, and strength" and they "love their neighbors as they love themselves." This dual love, as Charles Wesley sings, "Sanctifies, and makes us whole;" it "forms the Savior in the soul."

LIFE APPLICATION TOPIC: "GOD'S CHOSEN"

The Hebrew scriptures speak of a special relationship between God and those God delivered from slavery in Egypt. But these people, once downtrodden, have now forgotten that a bond with a liberating God brings with it the responsibility to never oppress others. Amos reminds them that their hoarding of peacetime wealth to build second homes at the expense of the poor will bring ruin. John Wesley believed that wealth is a gift of God in the hands of God's children—for in those hands money becomes food for the hungry. To be God's chosen is to live into an equitable relationship with others.

(See also the *Wesley Study Bible*: Wesleyan Core Term: "Discipline"; Life Application Topics: "God's Plan for You" and "Mission.")

* * * *

BIBLE STUDY EXTRA: MATTHEW AND THE GOSPEL OF MATTHEW

Matthew was one of the twelve apostles of Jesus. Because he appears closer to the end of the lists (seventh in Mark and Luke, eighth in Matthew and Acts), it seems that he was a disciple of lesser status. The Greek form of this name is derived from Hebrew or Aramaic, probably a shortened form of *mattithyah(u)*, meaning a "gift from God."

For much of church history, Matthew was thought to be a Jewish Christian believer writing for a Jewish Christian audience, perhaps around Syrian Antioch. And many early church leaders believed the Gospel of Matthew was originally written in Hebrew. More recent scholars have challenged this view, however. Although it is possible that Matthew was a Gentile Christian, almost nothing is known for sure about who he was or his intended audience.

The Gospel of Matthew has a long and distinguished history in the church. The connection between the Gospel and the apostle Matthew dates back to at least the middle of the second century A.D. Today, most scholars believe that Matthew is a revision of the Gospel of Mark, but in earlier times, early church fathers thought that Mark was a synopsis of Matthew.

Very soon after its completion, Matthew became the dominant account of the life and teaching of Jesus. One way this is documented is that Matthew was cited and commented upon more frequently, and it heads the lists in the manuscript copies of the four Gospels. Its early and widespread use is easy to understand because not only was its author considered to be one of Jesus' disciples, but it is carefully ordered and full of the sayings of Jesus in five major discourses, which made it ideal for teaching new believers (from *The New Interpreter's Dictionary of the Bible*, vol. 3, pp. 839–47).

REFLECTION QUESTIONS

1. Share what it means for you to be a part of your faith community. What does being committed to the church mean for you?

2. Think of a time when you stood up for what was right. Think of a time when you or someone you know wanted to stand up for what was right but either could not or would not. How did that situation change your relationship with that person?

3. When is it important to stand up for what is right? What is worth standing up for?

4. Consider what problems you are currently facing. Do you need help? How can you help others?

5. Disciplines are meant to help us grow deeper in faith and to enrich our relationship with God. Do you practice spiritual disciplines, for example, prayer, study, acts of justice and charity, or fasting? Decide to try a new discipline for two weeks.

6. Think of people you know who are kind and gracious. How do you feel when you are with them?

7. On a scale of one to ten (one being low and ten being high), how kind are you?

CHAPTER FOUR

AMAZING FAITH

At break of day, the king got up and hurried to
the den of lions. When he came near the den where
Daniel was, he cried out anxiously to Daniel, "O
Daniel, servant of the living God, has your God
whom you faithfully serve been able to deliver you
from the lions?" Daniel then said to the king, "O
king, live forever! My God sent his angel and shut
the lions' mouths so that they would not hurt me,
because I was found blameless before him; and
also before you, O king, I have done no wrong."
Then the king was exceedingly glad and com-
manded that Daniel be taken up out of the den. So
Daniel was taken up out of the den, and no kind
of harm was found on him, because he had trusted
in his God.

Daniel 6:19-23

* * * *

About a hundred years ago, right at the beginning of the twentieth century, a handsome young man named Clarence took his girlfriend on a summer outing. They took a picnic lunch out to a picturesque island in the middle of a small lake. She wore, as they did back in those modest days, a long dress with about a dozen petticoats. He was dressed in a suit with a high collar.

Clarence rowed them out to the island, dragged the boat onto shore, and spread their picnic supplies beneath a large shade tree. Clarence was so hypnotized by his girlfriend's beauty that he hardly noticed the hot sun on his face and the perspiration on his brow. Then Clarence's girlfriend softly whispered to him, "Clarence, you forgot the ice cream."

Clarence pulled the boat back to the water and rowed back to shore. He found a grocery store nearby, bought the ice cream, and then rowed back to the island. As he arrived back at the picnic site, Clarence's girlfriend batted her long eyelashes over deep blue eyes, and she purred, "Oh, Clarence, you forgot the chocolate syrup."

Well, love will make a person do amazing things. So Clarence got back into the rowboat

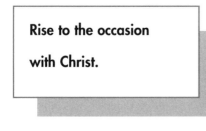

Rise to the occasion with Christ.

and returned to the store for syrup. As he rowed back toward the island, however, suddenly in the middle of the lake he stopped. Clarence sat there in the boat the rest of the afternoon, fascinated by an idea that had come into his mind. By the end of that afternoon, Clarence Evinrude had invented the outboard motor! And by the way, Clarence later married the girl who waited so long on the island.

That's what you call "rising to the occasion." That's what you call turning a problem into an opportunity, turning a challenge into a blessing, turning a defeat into a victory. And that's what great persons do.

That is precisely what Daniel did in Old Testament times, and that's why Daniel is one of the great heroes of the Bible. Remember the story with me.

Daniel and his people were thrust by the events of history into exile in a foreign land. Amazingly, like Joseph before him, because of his wisdom and spirit and his ability to interpret dreams, Daniel rose to a place of great leadership in this foreign kingdom. He became one of King Darius's top three advisors.

King Darius really liked Daniel, and he respected him immensely. But as sometimes happens in life, the other two top advisors became jealous of Daniel, so they

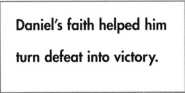

Daniel's faith helped him turn defeat into victory.

devised a cruel plot to get rid of him. They planned to use Daniel's faithfulness to God against him. They knew that three times every day Daniel knelt at his window and prayed to God, so deceitfully they persuaded King Darius to sign a new law proclaiming that if anybody bowed down before or prayed to anyone other than King Darius, that person would be thrown into a pit full of lions. Daniel was a person of deep faith, and even though he knew about this new law, he could not and would not deny his God, so Daniel continued his holy habit of praying to God.

The two jealous advisors saw Daniel praying, which was just what they were hoping for, and they reported his actions to the king. They also reminded the king about the new law and told the king he must follow through and cast Daniel into the lions' den or else he would look weak in the eyes of his people. King Darius was quite upset. He loved Daniel, but he felt that he had to go through with what the law demanded. He reluctantly sent Daniel to the lions' den, hoping that Daniel's God could save him.

King Darius could not sleep that night. He felt horrible about what he had been tricked into doing, and he was worried sick about Daniel, who by that time was in the lions' den. The next morning, King Darius rushed down to the pit, and he yelled out, "Daniel, are you okay? Has your God saved you?" The king was not really expecting an answer. He knew there was no way that Daniel could have survived a whole

night with those
hungry and fero-
cious lions. But
amazingly, a voice

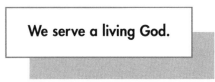

We serve a living God.

came up from the pit: "O king, live forever." It was Daniel's
voice. He was alive and well. Not a scratch on him. Daniel
came up out of the pit and explained to King Darius that his
God was the Lord of life and the Lord of creation and that
his God had protected him and watched over him and saved
him. He explained that he had trusted God because he knew
God loved him. King Darius was so amazed and so happy that
Daniel had survived, and he was so impressed by Daniel's faith
and Daniel's powerful, loving God, that he wrote a letter to all the
people of his kingdom encouraging them to bow down before
the God of Daniel. King Darius wrote about the God of Daniel
as the living God with the power to deliver and rescue and save.

Daniel is one of the great heroes of the Bible because he
had an unwavering faith in God. John Maxwell once said,
"A good leader knows the way, goes the way, and shows the
way." And that's what Daniel did.

Here are three things about Daniel's amazing faith:

1. DANIEL HAD THE SPIRITUAL STRENGTH TO *KNOW* THE WAY

Daniel knew the way for him was to keep praying to God,
even when his society said, "Don't do that!" We can find a

message there, and the message is that sometimes we have to stand our ground and refuse to follow the crowd. The majority is not always right.

Remember the story about the first graders who found a rabbit on the elementary school playground during recess one day. They brought the rabbit into their classroom and decided to adopt the rabbit as their class mascot. They wanted to name their new mascot, but they had a problem. They couldn't tell if their new class mascot was a boy rabbit or a girl rabbit. They took a vote and the majority voted that the rabbit was a boy rabbit, so they named him Ralph. This worked out fine until some weeks later Ralph gave birth to four baby bunnies!

The point is clear: there are some things you don't vote on because sometimes the majority voters are wrong.

Daniel realized that the majority isn't always right, and he stayed true to his faith in God. His strength came from many things, but one sure place was God's teachings. He knew God's teachings. He knew God's commandments. He took them to heart, and they became a part of his character. He knew, as the Bible puts it, that "we must obey God rather than any human authority" (Acts 5:29), and he took a stand in hard circum-stances, trusting

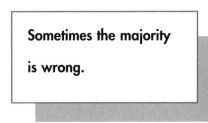

Sometimes the majority is wrong.

that God would be with him and that God would see him through. As we now know, God was with him, and God did see him through.

That's the first thing we see here: Daniel had the spiritual strength to know the way.

2. DANIEL HAD THE SPIRITUAL STRENGTH TO *GO* THE WAY

Even when circumstances, as unfair and unjust as they were, took him into the lions' den, Daniel went with courage, trusting God's faithfulness and promise to be with him.

But knowing and going are two different things.

Some years ago, I saw a man die unnecessarily because he refused to take penicillin. He believed that penicillin had the power to heal him, but for some strange reason, he was afraid to take it. The doctors reasoned with him. His wife and I begged him to take it. Other persons who had the experience of being saved by this miracle drug told him of their experience and how grateful they were for their heal-ing, but all to no avail. Every time they tried to ad-minister the peni-cillin, he would go into a panic attack

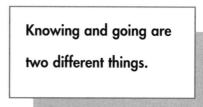

Knowing and going are two different things.

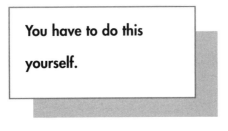

You have to do this yourself.

and adamantly refuse to take the medicine. Soon, the infection he was suffering in his body, which could have been knocked out by the penicillin, grew worse and worse. Eventually, he died, and it was all so unnecessary.

I would have gladly taken the medicine for him if I could have. So would his wife. But the bottom line was that we could not do it for him. We could not take his medicine for him. We could not take the leap of faith for him. We could not go the way of healing for him. He needed to do it, but for reasons known only to him, he just could not bring himself to do it, and he died!

Isn't that sad?

Isn't that tragic?

But the situation dramatically underscores a fundamental and basic tenet of faith: no one else can do it for you. No one else can make your personal faith commitment for you. Each one of us at some point must make her or his own leap of faith, her or his own commitment to love God and follow God's commands and serve God with strength and obedience and trust. It is not enough to know God's way. We have to stand on our own two feet and go God's way, knowing that God will go with us.

There's an old story about a man who was going to

attempt to ride a bicycle on a tightrope across Niagara Falls. Just before he started out, he turned to a stranger in the crowd of onlookers and said to him: "Do you believe I can make it across the Falls?"

"I sure do!" said the stranger.

"Okay then," said the biker, "jump on the handlebars!"

Do you and I trust God enough to jump on the handlebars and go the way of faith and trust in him?

Obviously, Daniel did, and this is what makes him one of the great heroes of the Bible. He had the amazing faith and wisdom to know the way, and he had the courage to go the way.

3. DANIEL ALSO HAD THE SPIRITUAL STRENGTH TO *SHOW* THE WAY

Because of his amazing faith, Daniel profoundly influenced others. People were drawn into the presence of God because of him.

The noted poet Edgar Guest expressed it powerfully in a poem he wrote many years ago, "Sermons We See":

I'd rather see a sermon than hear one any day,
I'd rather one should walk with me than merely show
    the way.

> —Edgar Guest, from *The Light of Faith*
> (Chicago: Reilly & Lee Co., 1926)

Sharing God's love will draw people to us.

So how is it with you? Do you *know* the way, *go* the way, and *show* the way?

A few years ago, I went into a nearby shop and ran into a member of our church. She was so excited because her daughter had just graduated from one of the finest universities in America. Proudly, that mom said of her daughter, "She could choose anywhere to live. She has done so well. She could start her career in any number of cities in America, but she's coming back to Houston because the thing she missed most while she was away in college was our church." The mother paused for a moment, and then she said, "Jim, do you know what she said to me the other day? She said, 'Mom, thank you for giving me God.'"

That's what a real hero does. He or she gives God to others. That's what all the great biblical heroes did: Abraham, Moses, David, Mary, Peter, Paul, and Daniel. But most of all, that's what Jesus does. He is alive and well. He gives us God.

Jesus, thank you for giving us God.

He gives us God's forgiveness; he gives us God's love; he gives us God's amazing grace.

* * * *

WESLEYAN CORE TERM: "LOVE OF NEIGHBOR"

The love of neighbor in the Wesleyan tradition grows out of one's relationship with God. All human affections and emotions are shaped by our relationship with God, and it is out of our relationship with God that we love our neighbor.

In Sermon 39: "Catholic Spirit," Wesley states that he believes it is possible for Christians to be united in heart, although it is not possible for us to be united in our thoughts or opinions. Wesley believed that the love of neighbor came first from a heart that was united, or right, with God. If one believes in God's goodness and in Jesus Christ, then Jesus is formed in our heart by faith. Thus, God's love for us and for all humankind dwells in us. As a result, we have energy and capacity for love of self, neighbor, and God. And we can dispense what Wesley calls the catholic spirit, or universal love.

LIFE APPLICATION TOPIC: "LEADERSHIP"

Humble, daring, discerning, empowering, and protecting: these are the characteristics of leadership.

With humility, Nehemiah weeps to align himself with God's purpose; he daringly risks his privileged life to do what is right. He discerns sad truths and hidden possibilities; motivates and equips the people for good work. Finally, he guards the boundaries of faith against all enemies within and without. Nehemiah is no mere program manager or property administrator. He grows leaders. He takes initiative but shares authority. He counts himself among the servants. Leaders are just cupbearers. The art is in knowing how the cup is to be filled, and to whom it should be carried.

(See also the *Wesley Study Bible*: Wesleyan Core Terms: "Lay Leadership," "Love of Neighbor," and "Love of the World"; Life Application Topics: "Not Making Another Stumble" and "Faith.")

* * * *

BIBLE STUDY EXTRA: DANIEL AND NEBUCHADNEZZAR

The tales of Daniel (Daniel 1–6) are set in the courts of Babylon and Persia. From his description, we learn that Daniel exemplified the virtues of wisdom, just judgment, and able leadership. Elsewhere in the Old Testament, we hear of a righteous man named Daniel (Ezekiel 14:14, 20). Evidently, he was considered a worthy Gentile because he is mentioned along with Job and Noah. Scholars generally regard Ezekiel's wise and righteous Daniel as the literary ancestor of the hero of the book of Daniel. Thus, from antiquity, Daniel was a revered hero's name.

Most scholars believe that Daniel in the biblical book of Daniel is a composite, fictional character and the stories about him probably originated in different times and places. What we have is an icon of Jewish piety of the second century B.C., an exemplar of steadfast faithfulness to God and the Law.

In chapter 1, four exiled Jewish youths are being trained at the Babylonian academy of wisdom for service at Nebuchadnezzar's royal court. There are two important Babylonian kings named Nebuchadnezzar. The second one is referred to here. He ruled for forty-three years, from 605 to 562 B.C. Nebuchadnezzar II's father, Nabopolassar, rebelled against Assyria and seized the throne, beginning a long struggle to drive Assyria from Babylonian territory.

It was only in the later stages of this struggle, following the destruction of Assyria and its replacement by Egypt as Babylon's main enemy, that Nebuchadnezzar appears in the biblical text. As the crown price, he defeated the Egyptian army that was celebrated by the prophet Jeremiah in an oracle against Pharaoh Neco (Jeremiah 46:1-12). However, later in 601, Nebuchadnezzar suffered severe losses in a bloody battle with Egypt on the Egyptian border, forcing Nebuchadnezzar to spend the following year refitting his army back in Babylon.

This defeat and the subsequent failure of the Babylonian army to march west in 600 B.C. provoked Jehoiakim to rebel. Then in 598, Nebuchadnezzar marched against Jerusalem. Jehoiakim died, leaving his son Jehoiachin to face the ensuing siege, which lasted three months. The king surrendered the city on March 15 or 16, 597 B.C. Subsequently, Jehoiachin, his mother, and the Judean elite were taken away into the Babylonian captivity and the vessels and treasures of the Temple were seized as booty.

As conqueror of Jerusalem and destroyer of the Temple, Nebuchadnezzar II was a ruler whose exploits were deeply seared into Jewish memory. Nebuchadnezzar's son, Amel-Marduk, later released Jehoiachin from prison (2 Kings 25:27; Jeremiah 52:31).

Hence the Nebuchadnezzar portrayed in Daniel appears to be a composite of several different rulers. Daniel conflates Nebuchadnezzar with Nabonidus, the last king of that dynasty. The traditions of Nebuchadnezzar's strange idol (Daniel 3) and of his sojourn in the wilderness (Daniel 4) appear to reflect negative Babylonian traditions about Nabonidus's religious innovation and his long sojourn in

Tema (from *The New Interpreter's Dictionary of the Bible*, vol. 4, pp. 245–46).

The first chapter of Daniel illustrates Daniel's determination to maintain his Jewish identity and moral freedom. From chapter 2, we see Daniel's skills as a sage and prophet. As a wise man, not only can he interpret the king's dream, but with God's help, he can also recall it—an accomplishment that even Joseph could not match (Genesis 41:1-36). As prophet, Daniel reveals an understanding of human history to its very end (Daniel 2:31-45). He successfully functions a second time as a dream interpreter in chapter 4, causing Nebuchadnezzar to offer praise to "the King of heaven" (v. 37). In chapter 5, Daniel outshines all the diviners of Babylon by interpreting to King Belshazzar the meaning of the handwriting on the wall. Then in chapter 6, a pious, brave, and trusting Daniel will not stop from praying three times each day even though by order of the Persian king, Darius, to do so means death by the lions.

The remaining six chapters report Daniel's inner and private history. Now Daniel becomes an apocalyptic visionary whom God empowers to tell the history of the future and the promise of resurrection (from *The New Interpreter's Dictionary of the Bible*, vol. 2, pp. 13–14).

REFLECTION QUESTIONS

1. Think of a person who knows the way of Christ. What have you learned from this person?

2. What are different ways you can go for God? In what ways is your church in mission? Commit to participating with your church on a mission trip.

3. Consider people you know who have shown you the way of Christ. Share how you became a Christian.

4. The amazing thing about faith in God is that it is dynamic; it can grow and shrink. Thinking about your spiritual life now, is it growing or shrinking? What can you do to refresh your faith in God?

5. What are five characteristics of leadership? List them. Which do you have? To which do you aspire? Pray about this.

6. We worship a living God; Jesus is alive and available to us today. Do you feel that you are alive in Christ?

CHAPTER FIVE

AMAZING CHURCH

I appeal to you therefore, brothers and sisters, by the mercies of God, to present your bodies as a living sacrifice, holy and acceptable to God, which is your spiritual worship. Do not be conformed to this world, but be transformed by the renewing of your minds, so that you may discern what is the will of God—what is good and acceptable and perfect.

Romans 12:1-2

* * * *

What's so great about the church? This seems to be a question that a lot of people are asking these days. I don't want to be overly emotional or too sentimental, but I would like to be very personal. Let me begin by telling you that I am sold on the church! I am committed to the church with all my heart! I believe in the church! I am immeasurably indebted to the church! Everything I have of any real, lasting value, I got from the church.

1. THE CHURCH GAVE ME MY UPBRINGING

The church began by giving me my upbringing, my early training. Now, I had a wonderful mother and father who filled our home with love, but in addition the church gave me another advantage—the greatest grandmother God ever made (not counting yours, of course). Grandmother lived with us. She loved the church so much, and I'm sure much of the deep love I have for the church today goes back to her and what I learned from her, just watching her love, serve, and appreciate the church. Whenever the church doors were open, she was there. Whatever they were doing down at the church, she supported it in every way.

She always loved her pastor. Our church was a small neighborhood church in Memphis. And although we never got the best preacher in the conference, she thought we had the best. Time and again, as pastors would come and go, I heard her say, "I believe this is the best one yet." And she would help the preachers get their message across. As we would go home from church, she would talk about the sermon, and she would say, "Wasn't that a great sermon!" or "Did you notice the wonderful thing the minister said about such and such?" Then one of us children would say, "But, Granny, he didn't say that." And she would answer, "Well, yes, but that's what he meant!"

She was always helping the preacher preach his sermon. I'm sure that the great respect and appreciation she had for her ministers planted a seed deep down inside of us children that later enabled both my brother and me to respond to God's call professionally as pastors and enabled my sister to become one of the finest lay leaders in the church I have ever known.

Going to church for Grandmother started on Saturday night. Each Saturday night, she read her Sunday school lesson and polished all of our shoes. And to this day, every time I put on my shoes to go to church I think of her and her devotion to God.

Once when I was six years old, she got me to help her with the shoes. The family teased me for years about what I did that Saturday night. I polished even the soles of the shoes! The family thought that was hilarious, but actually it made perfect sense to my six-year-old mind. I knew we were going to have Communion the next morning, and

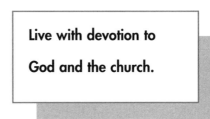

Live with devotion to God and the church.

I wanted the bottoms of our shoes to look good when we were kneeling at the altar! Grandmother instilled in me this intense sacredness about the church.

She believed in tithing. She believed that the first tenth belonged to the Lord. If you wanted to do more than that, it was nice, but that first tenth belonged to him. She didn't have much money. Sometimes we even talked to her about it and suggested that it would be all right to spend a little more on herself, but she never wavered in her sacrificial giving to the church. Every Sunday morning, she would call my brother, my sister, and me into the living room, and she would take our offering and tie it up in the corner of a white handkerchief, so we wouldn't lose it. And every year at Lent, she would get each of us children one of those Lenten giving books. You may remember them. They had a little pouch for each day of Lent that would hold a dime, and we would save our dimes to put into those little pouches so on Easter we could take a special offering to the church.

Also every Sunday morning, just when the preacher started to preach, she would slip each of us children some peppermint candy. I guess she thought that would help us make it through the sermon and keep our squirming to a minimum. She loved the church; and as the years passed and as we grew older, we realized that that's what made her what she was—that beautiful devotion to God and the church. What the church gave to her, she passed on to us.

It was a wonderful, special upbringing rooted deeply in the church.

2. THE CHURCH GAVE ME MY EDUCATION

I didn't have the money to go to college or seminary, but the church made it possible. A fine Methodist college, Lambuth University in Jackson, Tennessee, gave me a scholarship—an athletic-work scholarship. I played basketball and baseball, and I ran track. I cleaned up the gym. And I worked for the college recruitment office. Through that office, I organized a group of singers—we called ourselves "The Eight Freshmen"—and with my baritone ukulele, we would go out in the name of the college and perform at high school assemblies. Then we would tell them about our school and encourage them to come to our college.

Then when I got to seminary, I served two churches and worked as a janitor on the campus. But in addition, a men's Bible class in a Methodist church in Columbus, Ohio, gave me a scholarship that paid all my tuition for three years. The church made it possible for me to get an education— an education designed to teach me not only how to make a living but also how to make a life!

Living, learning, and making a life.

3. THE CHURCH GAVE ME A WONDERFUL FAMILY

Then, too, the church has given me a wonderful family. We have been so blessed, so fortunate. Our life together has centered in the church, and that would have been true even if I were not a professional minister. When you stop to think about it, the church is meant to always be there for us, isn't it? That is dramatically symbolized by the altar. I'm so glad that we have an altar in our church and that we come to the altar at the special moments of life. Think of it:

- We bring our babies here for baptism.
- People, especially youth, come here to claim Christ as Savior and to confirm the Christian faith as their own choice of a lifestyle.
- We come here to get married.
- We come here when someone we love dies.
- We come here when we are happy and when we are sad.
- We come here when we are sick and when we get well.
- We come here to cry.
- And we come here to worship.

God can meet us anywhere, but sometimes we are most receptive at his altar.

* * * *

Time and again over the years, our family has come to the church altar—in our joys and sorrows. The church has always been there for us. My wife and I are also so proud of our children. They have brought such gladness into our lives. Sometimes I think they were just born good, but then I know better. I know that they are what they are because we, as parents, have had a lot of help from the church and from God. Then, too, the church has given me a wonderful career, many, many warm friendships, much happiness, and a sense of meaning and fulfillment.

So you can see that I am sold on the church. The great thing is that many others who have been close to the church over the years could give a similar witness because there is no institution in the world that serves people like the church. There is no institution in the world that helps families like the church. There is no institution in the world that redeems lives like the church. There is no institution in the world that teaches love like the church. There is no institution in the world that lifts God up like the church. That's what's so great about the church!

> **There is no institution that serves people like the church.**

* * * *

A few years ago, a Gallup Poll revealed some highly significant things about people who are highly committed to the church. The survey revealed the following:

1. The highly committed group was far happier than the general population. Sixty-eight percent rated themselves as very happy. They demonstrated a greater satisfaction with life.
2. In the highly committed group, family life was far stronger.
3. The highly committed group tended to be more loving, more understanding, and more tolerant of people of different races and religions than the general population. They were far more accepting of others.
4. The people highly committed to the church were far more involved in working with the community to improve the quality of life than the uncommitted or nominally committed group. Almost 50 percent of this highly committed group worked in some way with poor, homeless, or older people, or those who, in some manner, were rejected by society.

That's what's so great about the church!

That's why in Romans 12, the apostle Paul challenges us to give our bodies—that means all that we have and all that

we are—to God
and his church as a
living sacrifice. He
believed that the
church is the
guardian of God's
truth, the advocate

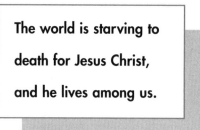

The world is starving to death for Jesus Christ, and he lives among us.

of God's forgiveness, the proclaimer of God's word, the instrument of God's healing, the fellowship of God's redeemed people, the sanctuary for God's worship. What's so great about the church? So many things, I couldn't even begin to list them all.

Let me just underscore one more, the one that sums it all up. What's so great about the church? Simply this: the church has Jesus Christ! The world is starving to death for Jesus Christ, and he lives among us. He is God's message and messenger rolled up into one, and the church has him. No other institution even claims to have him. No other institution or movement or organization has anything that even comes close or that even begins to compare with Jesus Christ. No other institution or movement or organization can share Christ with a needy world like the church.

Sure, we fall short. Sure, we fail and make mistakes. And sure, too often, we quarrel and quibble over things that really don't matter. But this is the bottom line: we are here to share Jesus Christ with a needy world, and everything we do is for that purpose. We have worship services; we have

Sunday school classes; we have prayer groups, support groups, Bible study groups, youth groups, children's groups, singles groups, and mission work groups. We take trips, we put on dramas, we play games, we present concerts, we paint houses, we build clinics, we feed the hungry, and we help the needy—all for one purpose, so we can share the love of Jesus Christ, so we can tell people about him.

This is our purpose.

Steve Goodier tells the story of two warriors, Cyrus and Cagular. Cyrus, of course, was the noted emperor of Persia. Cagular was a little-known but courageous chieftain whose troops tore the Persian army apart time and time again as they resisted Cyrus's attempts to expand his southern border. Finally, Cyrus amassed his whole army, surrounded Cagular, captured him, and brought him to the capital for trial and execution.

On the day of the trial, Cagular and his family were brought to the judgment chamber. Cagular, the young chieftain, faced the throne. He was six feet tall and looked every inch the nobleman. Cyrus, the emperor, was duly impressed.

"What would you do should I spare your life?" the emperor asked.

"Your majesty," replied the warrior, "if you spared my life, I would return home and remain your obedient servant as long as I live."

"What would you do if I spared the life of your wife?" Cyrus questioned.

"Your majesty, if you spared the life of my wife, I would die for you."

So moved was Cyrus, the emperor, by Cagular's answer that he freed Cagular and his wife and appointed the chieftain to be governor of the southern province.

On the trip home, Cagular was excited, and he enthused to his wife, "Did you notice the marble entrance to the palace? Did you see the elegant corridor to the throne room? And did you see the chair on which he sat? It was made of one lump of solid gold!"

His wife appreciated her husband's excitement but admitted, "I didn't really notice any of that."

"Well," Cagular asked in amazement, "what did you see?"

She looked seriously into his eyes and said tenderly, "I beheld only the face of the man who said he would die for me."

What's so great about the church? It's that in our better moments we lift up and hold high the face of him who loved us so much that he would die for us.

> **The church holds high the face of Jesus, who loved us so much that he died for us.**

* * * *

WESLEYAN CORE TERM: "CHURCH"

Chapter 14 of 1 Corinthians reminds us that even the most mysterious spiritual gifts are subject to an utterly pragmatic standard: Does this spiritual gift build up the church? John Wesley noted that usefulness was the criterion for determining the value of all gifts. "By this alone are we to estimate all our gifts and talents" (Notes, 1 Corinthians 14:5). The appeal to usefulness raises the question, "Useful toward what goal?" The chapter mentions the "building up" of the church, but what does that mean? The first verse provides an answer. "Pursue love and strive for the spiritual gifts." As Christians imitate Christ and grow in love in the church community, they are built up together into holiness. Growth in love must be "pursued." Commenting on verse 1, John Chrysostom compares pursuing love with hunting. "He that is in chase beholds that only which is chased, and towards that he strains himself, and leaves not off until he lay hold of it" (*Homily* 35).

LIFE APPLICATION TOPIC: "FRIENDSHIP"

David and Jonathan provide us with perhaps the most intriguing story of friendship in the Bible. Theirs was a relationship of loyalty, trust, and support. Every time we read this story it leads to the question: What kind of friend am I? A true friend is one who, during our darkest hours, offers hope, encouragement, and support. Our emotional stability is predicated on whether we have someone who is willing to stand with us and sometimes behind us to push us over the hump of despair. That's the kind of friend we all ought to strive to be.

(See also the *Wesley Study Bible*: Wesleyan Core Terms: "Connection," "Women's Leadership," and "Personal Holiness"; Life Application Topics: "Family," "Caring for the Poor," "Caring for the Outcast," and "Christian Household.")

* * * *

BIBLE STUDY EXTRA: ROMANS

The Letter to the Romans is the longest letter written by Paul the apostle, and it is also one of the most important for the church. According to the introduction of the Letter to the Romans in the *Wesley Study Bible* (p. 1367), Romans is widely regarded as Paul's most theologically important writing and contains Paul's mature reflections on Christian faith and ministry. This letter's impact on Christians, especially the doctrine of justification by faith, is enormous. Its influence on John Wesley is evident throughout his writing, most famously in this journal entry:

> In the evening I went very unwillingly to a society in Aldersgate Street, where one was reading Luther's Preface to the Epistle to the Romans. About a quarter before nine, while he was describing that change which God works in the heart through faith in Christ, I felt my heart strangely warmed. I felt I did trust in Christ, Christ alone for salvation, and an assurance was given me that he had taken away *my* sins, even *mine*, and saved *me* from the law of sin and death. (*Works*, "Journals," May 24, 1738, par. 14)

But why did Paul write such a lengthy and dense letter to a Christian community, one that he had never visited before? Unfortunately, the letter itself gives no explicit answer. The closest it comes to a purpose is given in Romans 15:15, where Paul claims that he has written quite boldly "by way of reminder." Although this is not much information, it does make the reader turn back to the letter and study its nature and the directions of its logical flow.

As with all of his letters, Paul works out of a basic sense of the development of God's plan of salvation over time. Scripture, for Paul, told a story in which creation; the fall into sin; the establishment of Israel and the giving of the Law; Israel's failure, marked by the exile; and the prophetic hope for national and universal renewal were the defining moments. Paul's theological task is to attach the new and climactic event in salvation history, the coming of the Messiah, to that history. So in Romans, Paul strikes a careful balance between continuity and discontinuity in this history of salvation. God's new work in Christ is tied firmly to Old Testament promise (Romans 1:2; 3:21; 9–11; 15:9-12) at the same time as it is presented as a new work that takes place outside the realm of the Law and the covenant it represents. Paul asserts that Christ is the "end" of the Law, the word *end* probably having a sense of climax: Christ ends the Law by bringing what it has been pointing toward all along (from *The New Interpreter's Bible Dictionary*, vol. 4, pp. 841–49).

REFLECTION QUESTIONS

1. Share what your church means to you. In what ways does your church reflect God to its congregation and the wider community and world? Where does your church need to change?

2. Name three people you love, and share why.

3. In what ways do you serve God through your church? Are there other places or ways in which you would like to serve?

4. How faithful are you, your family, and your church to God's mission to go into the world and make disciples of Jesus Christ?

5. Commit to pray for your church pastor(s) and leaders every day for the next two weeks.

6. Make a list of ten people who do not attend a church anywhere, and pray for them daily for the next year.

7. What is the most amazing thing about your family, your church, your community?

CHAPTER SIX

AMAZING SURPRISES

Jacob left Beer-sheba and went toward Haran.
He came to a certain place and stayed there for the
night, because the sun had set. Taking one of the
stones of the place, he put it under his head and lay
down in that place. And he dreamed that there was
a ladder set up on the earth, the top of it reaching to
heaven; and the angels of God were ascending and
descending on it. And the LORD stood beside him
and said, "I am the LORD, the God of Abraham
your father and the God of Isaac; the land on which
you lie I will give to you and to your offspring; and
your offspring shall be like the dust of the earth, and
you shall spread abroad to the west and to the east
and to the north and to the south; and all the families of the earth shall be blessed in you and in your
offspring. Know that I am with you and will keep

you wherever you go, and will bring you back to this land; for I will not leave you until I have done what I have promised you." Then Jacob woke from his sleep and said, "Surely the LORD is in this place— and I did not know it!" And he was afraid, and said, "How awesome is this place! This is none other than the house of God, and this is the gate of heaven."

Genesis 28:10-17

* * * *

Some years ago, a young man went out to West Texas to work on a ranch one summer. It seemed like a good idea at the time—a great way to spend the summer and to make some money to help with his college expenses. He had seen pictures of the ranch. It looked exotic and exciting, and the thought of being a cowboy for an entire summer made him feel macho and full of adventure. But when his parents drove him out there, he was so disappointed when he saw the ranch. He was so let down, so disillusioned. It wasn't anything like what he had pictured. It was run by a middle-aged couple and located way back in the hills, remote, cut off from civilization—nothing around. Even the nearest Dairy Queen was seventy-nine miles away. It was a desolate, gloomy, lonely place.

He didn't want to stay but he had signed a contract,

> **We can find something good in an unexpected place.**

so he felt that he had to stay—at least for a while. His parents fretted and fidgeted all the way home, and he cried himself to sleep that night. His first few letters home were sad and pitiful. But then during the second week of the summer, something happened to change all that—the daughter of the rancher came home from college. His letters began to pick up. Soon he was describing that ranch as the most beautiful spot he had ever seen in his life, and by September they could hardly get him home to start back to school!

He had found something good in an unexpected place. When you stop and think about it, this is a common experience in life—finding something good in an unexpected place. For example, a couple of weeks ago, I put on one of my suits that I had not worn in several months. I put my hand in the right-hand coat pocket, and there was a twenty-dollar bill! I didn't remember leaving it there, but there it was and it made me feel so good! In fact, I think I spent about a hundred dollars that week just thinking about that twenty-dollar bill. I just spent it over and over and over!

Now, of course, that wonderful surprise of finding something good in an unexpected place is a great feeling, a thrilling happening. The Scriptures are full of that kind of experience. And more often than not, in the Bible that something good found in that unexpected place is none other than God himself.

Time and again, we see it in the Scriptures:

- Moses, brooding in the desert, finds God there in a burning bush.
- Isaiah, in Babylon with his exiled people, finds God in a strange land.
- Job, in the midst of deep pain and tragic calamity, finds God in his woeful circumstances.
- Elijah, lying under a broom tree, wallowing in self-pity, thinking suicidal thoughts, then of all things, finds God there.
- Saul of Tarsus, on a vigilante hunt, looking for Christians to persecute and kill, finds instead the risen Lord.

And then, talk about God in unexpected places—look at Golgotha! Who would imagine that you could find God in a crucifixion, on a cross? But look! Surprise of surprises—he is there! And surprise of surprises, he is here too!

Finding God in unexpected places is precisely what Genesis 28 is all about. Jacob says it for us powerfully, "Surely the LORD is

> **Surely the LORD is in this place—and I did not know it.**

in this place—and I did not know it." Can you identify with Jacob as he speaks these time-honored words? Can you relate to what he is feeling when he utters these words in a tone of hushed reverence? Has God ever surprised you like that? Where have you found yourself thinking, *Surely the Lord is in this place, and I did not know it?*

Do you remember the context of this great verse? Jacob is on the lam. He is running for his life. Through deceit and trickery, through plotting, lying, and conniving, he has stolen away his brother's birthright. And he has been found out. Now he is running away because he is scared to death of his brother, Esau. On the first night of his escape, he dreams of a ladder going up into heaven. There, God speaks to him and makes a covenant with him to watch over him. "Wherever you go, whatever you do," says the Lord, "I will be there. I will be with you."

Jacob is in a tough situation. Weighed down with fear and guilt, struggling with remorse, he is anxious, lonely, confused, and ashamed. And suddenly God is there—even there. Then Jacob says these words that have resounded across the centuries, words that have become one of the greatest statements of faith in all the Bible, "Surely the LORD is in this place—and I did not know it."

Let's be more specific. Let's bring this closer to home by asking, What are some of the surprising and unexpected places where we might find God? There are many. Let me suggest a few, and I'm sure you will think of others.

1. IN THE UNEXPECTED PLACE OF STRESS

Jacob was stressed out by his problems. Sometimes the problems and tensions and stresses of life simply overwhelm us. We can see no way out, and then suddenly God is there, bringing peace to our stretched nerves and troubled souls.

It happened in a most unlikely place—a stressful administrative board meeting in a Methodist church in the Midwest. I was the pastor of that little church, and I was dreading that night. More than words can express, I dreaded it. I had lost sleep dreading it. I was stressed out over it. We were going to have a knock-down, drag-out meeting that night. I knew it was coming. I had been forewarned.

Fred Jones had hurt feelings, and he was coming to disrupt the meeting. He was mad at Dick Richards, and he was going to unleash his anger at the board meeting that Wednesday night. We had just completed a new education building. We were making plans to open and dedicate the new building, but Fred Jones was determined to stop us!

Why? Well, it was really very simple: his feelings were hurt. He had been on every building project committee at the church for forty years, but somehow this time he had been left off this committee for this project. He was hurt and angry. He felt unneeded, left out. For months, while the education building was going up, Fred had been seething. He was especially upset with Dick Richards, who was chairperson of the building committee.

Fred Jones was convinced that everything had been done wrong and that the building was hazardous for our children. He had personally inspected the building and was coming to the board meeting to block the opening of the new educational wing. He had a long list of grievances. He had a long list of what he considered to be glaring errors made by the committee. He had an even longer list of things that Dick Richards had done that Fred considered wrong, unsafe, and illegal. Fred was upset, and talk about a stressful, horrible situation, he did take it out on the board that night.

It was terrible. He attacked Dick. Dick fought back. Voices were raised. People began to choose sides. Tension was heavy in the room. Jealousy, envy, resentment, and pettiness were ruling the night. Finally, the board chairperson got so flustered by the whole thing that he tried to resolve it by calling for a vote. He said, "Everyone for Fred's side, raise your hand." But then came a voice from the back of the room: "Wait a minute, Mr. Chairman. Before we vote on anything, I want to say something." It was Laura Benson. With tears glistening in her eyes, Laura Benson stood up and began to speak. My, how she spoke!

"What is all this talk about sides?" she said. "What is all this talk about Fred's side and Dick's side? We are a church! We don't choose sides. We are all on the same side. We are all on God's side! We are a family here—God's family! Sides? It breaks my heart to hear us squabble like this. It must break God's heart too!"

With that, Laura Benson sat down, and there was not a sound in the room. In the silence, we realized that she was right. We were all ashamed of how we had been acting. Then Fred Jones stood up. Nervously, he cleared his throat, and softly, he spoke. "I'm so sorry," he said, "and I want to apologize to all of you, but especially to Dick. I don't know what got into me. Maybe I was jealous, maybe I felt left out, but thanks to Laura, I know now that I was wrong—and I'm sorry."

Then Fred walked over to Dick Richards, extended his hand, and quietly said, "Dick, can you ever forgive me?" Dick stood, shook Fred's hand, and then, smiling through his tears,

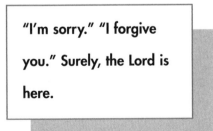

"I'm sorry." "I forgive you." Surely, the Lord is here.

he pulled Fred forward and gave Fred a big bear hug. All the board members stood and applauded. And then they all began hugging one another, and I just stood there and watched the Holy Spirit work. I thought, *How beautiful is the picture of reconciliation.* And under my breath I muttered with a sigh of relief, "Surely the Lord is in this place, and I did not know it." Amazingly, we can find God in the unexpected place of stress.

2. IN THE UNEXPECTED PLACE OF SORROW

It seems that it would be easy to find God in beautiful, sacred, loved places, or in those situations where the breaks are going our way; but the truth is that God is never nearer to us than when we are hurting. Time after time, I have heard people say it: "This is the hardest thing we've ever gone through. Our hearts are broken, but we will be all right because God is with us as never before."

One little boy put it like this: "Why are all the vitamins in spinach and not in ice cream where they belong?" I don't know. We'll have to ask God about that, but vitamins *are* in spinach, and God is uniquely and especially with us in the wilderness of sorrow. I think I know why. I think the reason we find God so powerfully in the unexpected place of sorrow is that God is like a loving parent who wants to be especially close to his children when they are in pain.

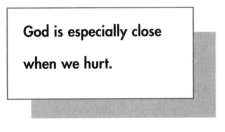

God is especially close when we hurt.

Some months ago, I was at the hospital visiting a little girl who was very sick. Her mother had been at her bedside for days and days. The doctor called me out into the hallway and asked me to see if I could get that young mother to go home for a while. He said, "She hasn't slept, hasn't eaten for several days. She has got to be exhausted. See if you can get her to go home."

I went back to the room and said to her, "Tricia, why don't you let me take you home for a while?"

She looked up at me and said, only as a mother can, "Jim, you don't really want me to leave her when she is this sick, do you?"

Being a parent myself, I understood and said to her, "No, I'll go downstairs and get you a sandwich."

God is like that—a loving parent who wants to be especially close to his children when they are hurting. Isn't it something how God shows up in the most surprising, unexpected places of stress and sorrow?

3. IN THE UNEXPECTED PLACE OF DISAPPOINTMENT

Some years ago, a friend of mine who has served as a missionary in a remote part of Africa for many years told me a true story that touched my heart. A talented and dedicated brother-and-sister missionary team came to his mission station in Africa. Both the brother and the sister were doctors. They had come there to fulfill a lifelong dream of theirs—being medical missionaries. They told of playing together in the backyard of their home as they were growing up and how they would pretend to be medical missionaries. And now their dream had come true. However, not too long after they arrived in Africa, the brother became sick. Some tests were run, and the news was not good. He had about a fifty-fifty chance of surviving his illness.

His sister called my missionary friend. He came to her quickly. She explained the situation to him and said, "I don't know how to tell him. I wanted you to come and help me tell him." Together they decided to just show him his medical chart, to hand him the chart and let him read it for himself.

"Are the tests back?" he asked. "Is everything all right?"

His sister handed him the medical report. He skimmed over it quickly. At first he grimaced, but then he said to his sister: "Don't cry, Jennie. Look. This gives us a wonderful opportunity. We came out here to show these people how great the Christian faith is. Now we can show them, really show them how Christians handle trouble. That's all that matters about trouble—how you handle it. And now we have the unique opportunity to show them how Christians handle adversity." Then he said, "If I survive this, I'll serve

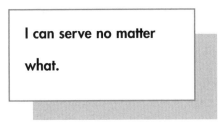

I can serve no matter what.

God here. If not, I'll serve God in heaven. Either way, I win!"

God can be found at the altar of the church. God can be found in the Scriptures. God can be found in prayer, in worship services, in Sunday school classes, and in spiritual retreats. But thank God, he can also be found in the surprising, unexpected places of stress, of sorrow, and of disappointment. Surely God is in those places too. And we can know it, and we can claim his strength!

* * * *

WESLEYAN CORE TERM: "MEANS OF GRACE"

John Wesley taught that our becoming and growing as Christians is enabled by grace. Through grace, we are invited into a transforming relationship with God, which largely takes place as we participate in the means of grace The means of grace are practices that the Holy Spirit uses to either draw us to God (prevenient grace) or enable us to know our sins are forgiven (justification) and grow in love for God and our neighbor (sanctification). Means of grace include the devotional reading of Scripture, prayer, fasting, the

Lord's Supper, Christian conversation, and acts of compassion and service to our neighbors. It is in the means of grace that we encounter the presence of God in all its transforming and loving power. As we faithfully participate in means of grace through worship, sacraments, daily devotions, fellowship, and service, God enables us to increasingly recover the divine image of love in which we were created.

LIFE APPLICATION TOPIC: "GOD'S REDEEMING LOVE"

It's a shocking story. The woman Hosea loves is a guilty whore, just as guilty as the woman they bring to Jesus who had been caught in adultery (John 8:3). Neither woman deserves the love and forgiveness they are given, but both are released from their past and offered a new life. Charles Wesley never got over the shocking news of the "stupendous love of God most high . . . full of unutterable grace" that meets us in our sin, forgives our past, and calls us to a new life. Wesley stretched adjectives to describe it. Experience that love and nothing is the same again.

(See also the *Wesley Study Bible*: Wesleyan Core Terms: "Grace," "Redemption," and "Self-Denial"; Life

Application Topics: "Disappointment," "Suffering," and "Restoration.")

* * * *

BIBLE STUDY EXTRA: BEERSHEBA

The city of Beersheba was part of the territorial inheritance of Simeon and is described as the southernmost city of the land of Israel. In the Bible, the name *Beersheba* means "well of seven" or "well of the oath." These meanings are explained by two narratives, both of which underscore the potential danger for the biblical patriarchs when negotiating in a new land. In one, duplicitous Philistine servants challenge Abraham, even though he had legitimately negotiated for water rights. Abraham's insistence and savvy, however, protect him as he offers seven lambs to Abimelech, and thus, the two swear a binding oath before the powerful king's army commander, Phicol (Genesis 21:30-33). A similar account is repeated in the next generation, as Isaac must renegotiate the settlement with the same king and commander. This time, Isaac's servants dig their own well, solidifying Isaac's rightful claim (Genesis 26:33).

Beersheba is portrayed as the spiritual and physical home of the patriarchs in other ways. Abraham is said to have lived there after God tested him with Isaac (Genesis 22:19). It served as Jacob's home before he departed to Haran to flee Esau's murderous revenge (Genesis 28:10). Although the narratives of Genesis do not specify that God saved the patriarchs from these situations, their successful escapes and negotiations underscore the hidden hand of God, who repeatedly rescues them and to whom they respond in worship.

Abraham calls upon "the name of the LORD, the Everlasting God [El Olam]" in Beersheba and plants a tamarisk tree, perhaps to mark the religious center (Genesis 21:33). Isaac receives a reassurance of promise and blessing from God there, to which he responds by building an altar (Genesis 26:23-25). Similarly, Jacob offers sacrifices to the God of Abraham before he continues to Egypt, where he and his family escape famine (Genesis 46:1, 6).

In addition, the wilderness of Beersheba becomes a place where the divine presence may be encountered. In Beersheba's vicinity Hagar wanders with Ishmael before God intervenes to save their lives (Genesis 21:14). In a later generation, the prophet Elijah first stops in Beersheba when he escapes Jezebel's plan to have him killed. There, Elijah is protected by an angel before he continues his journey to Mount Horeb, where he witnesses a theophany (1 Kings 19:1-18).

Samuel's sons are also identified as being judges there, pointing to Beersheba's importance as an administrative center (1 Samuel 8:2). Perhaps it was the association of Beersheba as the place where the patriarchs offered sacrifice that led to its reputation as a religious center. Individuals apparently made pilgrimages to Beersheba, but by the time of Amos (eighth century B.C.), it already had the reputation for being dominated by foreign worship practices (Amos 5:5). Because of the associated idolatry, Amos condemns individuals who worship at Beersheba as those who abandon their obligation to God (Amos 8:14; from *The New Interpreter's Dictionary of the Bible*, vol. 1, p. 419).

REFLECTION QUESTIONS

1. Where are the stress, sorrow, and disappointments in your life now?

2. What Bible passages are especially helpful to you when you need a good word from God?

3. Think of a time when you needed to offer your forgiveness to someone. What prompted you to forgive that person? Think of a time when someone offered forgiveness to you for something you did.

4. Share the last time you felt close to Christ.

5. What are some ways that you can ease conflict and promote understanding in your daily life?